Pool Hustlers: The Legend of English Dan

Pool Hustlers: The Legend of English Dan

Ramel Self

Copyright © 2017 Ramel Self
All rights reserved.

ISBN: 1537163876
ISBN 13: 9781537163871

Preface

POOL HUSTLERS: THE LEGEND OF ENGLISH DAN IT IS VERY IMPORTANT TODAY that we capture, and share some of the many moments of yesterday. I wrote this book, to do just that. For those who are old enough to remember, and have witnessed this era of *high stakes pool hustlers*, I envy you. For everyone else, I hope this book will stimulate your imagination, and allow your inner vision to take a peek into their fascinating world.

About 35 years ago, I was fortunate to be in the company of a few of English Dan's pool shooting associates. When they spoke of his extraordinary skills, their eyes danced with excitement. Their praises, and accolades bubbled over the top like champagne. As I listened to these grown men tell giddy stories of that magical era, I made a mental note to myself... "These tales have all the making of a very good book". So about 3 years ago, I know what you are thinking, "Why did it take 30 years?" I've been busy. Nonetheless, I sat down with Mr. English Dan, now well into his 80's, and still as sharp as ever. I bought a half dozen spiral notebooks, and a dozen No.2 pencils, (never quite learned how to type) and began to pick his brain and asked him to revisit events that took place over 60 years ago.

I am forever indebted to my personal assistant, Lisa Harris for transcribing my sometimes illegible notes. Had I typed them myself, the book would be another 30 years. I then asked the very talented artist, Ms. Keisha Whately, to recreate those memorable pool hall scenes. I am also compelled to thank Ms. LaDeva Davis, the beautiful daughter of pool hall owner, Chick Davis, for some original timeless photos of her beloved father. His pool hall in South Philadelphia, as well as other pool halls in the inner cities and throughout the United States, became the stage for an odd collaboration of artists and artisans. Their canvas was the green felt, and their brushes were pool cues, and the result was masterpieces.

A special thanks to my wife, Cyncere for your eternal support.

BROAD AND SOUTH STREETS, PHILADELPHIA, PA 1952

Broad and South Streets, Philadelphia, PA 1952

English Dan

CHAPTER 1

For The Love of The Game

THE SMOKE-FILLED POOL ROOM LOCATED near Broad and South Streets, was unlike any other in the city. It was perched right in the center of South Philadelphia's nightspots. Pep's Musical Bar was a world renowned locale and entertainment venue for some of the world's famous jazz and blues performers. The club was always buzzing with the likes of Dizzy Gillespie, John Coltrane and BB King.

However, tonight the focus was across the street at Chick's Pool Hall. Chick Davis was a young black entrepreneur in a city where there were few. His success won the attention and the gratitude of all the people, rich and poor, black and white. His pool hall became an instant success, and attracted some of the area's best pool shooters.

Tonight would not be any different, not only were these two shooters the very best, there was no love lost between them. The pool match that had everyone talking about, was between PJ, the trash talking, hard shooting gangster from South Philly, and the slim, smooth pool shooter from North Philly, named *English Dan*.

As the crowd filed into the pool hall to get good standing spots, close to the center table, everyone was anticipating who would win this highly publicized match. They were also wondering, if more than a pool match may occur. It was no secret that PJ did not take losing lightly, and English Dan very seldom lost.

Chick's Pool Hall was nestled on Rodman Street off of Broad Street. It was a medium-size pool hall with about 10 tables and the center table was always covered and reserved for those special matches. It was a very popular pool hall attracting the entire range of players and bettors. On any given day, you could find a match being played for anywhere between one dollar a game to one thousand dollars a game. This particular match was truly special; it was being played for a total of $5,000.00, a staggering figure unheard of in 1952. Chick always demanded a 3% cut from the high-stakes matches. It was a fee he used to keep the place in tip top condition, and also to take care of his "friend" on the Police Department. No one griped about the "tax" because they could always go there and hustle pool in a safe atmosphere. Tonight would yield Chick $300 and because of the magnitude and sensitivity of the match, Chick asked his friend, Detective Washington to be on hand.

PJ arrived first after parking his sparkling black Lincoln. He strutted into the pool hall with his cue stick and a small paper bag. Everyone in South Philly knew PJ, and everyone respected him. However, lately the respect began to turn into fear, as stories of his malicious acts made people stay out of his way. PJ was born Peter Joseph Anderson, in 1925 to a well-to-do family in South Philly. The family had a few legitimate business and a few that were not. Peter Joseph, a name he always hated to be called, gravitated towards the illegitimate side of the family businesses.

The Anderson family had about five successful grocery stores throughout South Philly; that also doubled as a front for their number writing enterprise. Once the numbers racket migrated from

New York, the Andersons were one of the first black families that benefited from this illegal gold mine. The street lottery would catch on like wildfire, and anyone remotely connected to this business would prosper. PJ was a fairly smart kid, and did pretty well in school. By the time he reached junior high school, he was helping out in the grocery stores, but he immediately found that boring. He pleaded with his father to let him help out with the numbers game. His father protested the move; however, after allowing PJ to handle a few of the minor operations, it was apparent where Peter Joseph would make his mark.

The Anderson family was so successful, that one of the high ranking Capos, personally oversaw their operation. Lieutenants usually handle such matters, but Luigi Appellini liked PJ's father, and how he ran his businesses. *Louie Apples,* as some of his close associates called him, took a liking to PJ. When World War II broke out in December 1941 many young black men enlisted, however Peter Joseph Senior felt his son could serve him better here at home. When the selective service qualified young Peter 1A, Louie Appellini's connections had him disqualified 1F. The father was grateful for the gesture, however the senior Anderson knew that favors in this life, were never without consequences.

There was not a lot of spare time for a young man rising up in the ranks of the family business. PJ hung out with a few girlfriends every chance he got, but his true passion was shooting pool. PJ started shooting around the age of 13, by the time he turned 16, PJ was very, very good. There were not many *black halls* in South Philly, so when his reputation out grew the neighborhood pool halls, PJ began to venture into the *white* pool halls. This was a time when going into a white neighborhood to play an innocent game of basketball was dangerous. Imagine the danger of walking into a pool hall full of white men and gracefully and strategically stripping their best shooters of their egos and even more damaging, their cash. This was only possible because of his family connection with Louie Appellini. PJ knew this, and he also knew that all the connections in the world would not stop the rage of an angry white man, that just lost a week's wages to a young pool shooting nigger. So he didn't venture down that path too often. However, as he once said "It was sure a lot of fun!"

Chick's pool hall was just about bulging at the seams when one of PJs boys yells across the room "Hey PJ when in the hell is the cat from North Philly coming? You gotta make quick work of this sucker, we gotta go hangout after this ass-whipping!" PJ just smiled because he knew this cat from North Philly would not be quick work. PJ was very confident with his pool shooting ability but he knew this cat, English Dan was something special.

English Dan was born Eddie Gordon and the first time he picked up a cue stick, he said it *felt magical.* He said, "It was like an extension of his human anatomy." Dan was a nickname he picked up as a young child. "English" is a slang term for controlling the cue ball (the white one) by hitting it in various spots to dictate where the ball will travel and where the ball will stop. The first time Eddie walked into the pool hall on Broad and Susquehanna Avenue it was electric. His senses danced at the sight, the sounds and even the smell of the pool hall. He was about 12 years old and the older cats tried to run him off, but Eddie was like a magnet. At first he just watched for a few visits, then one day when the hall was not busy, Eddie picked a cue and played his first game. He destroyed the guy. It was as if he had been playing pool, all of his young life. Eddie began to shoot every day, and sometimes he would hookie school just to hang out in the pool halls. Eddie and a few of his friends began to frequent the pool halls so much the truant officers knew where to come to round them up. Eddie was slender and tall for his age. By the time he reached 16, he looked like a young man and the truant officers eventually stopped harassing him. That's when his real education began.

There were no family businesses for Eddie and his older brother, John. Their parents, Nancy and John Sr., worked hard for their modest lifestyle. They lived in a humble apartment on Diamond Street near 20th. John, his older brother of 3 years joined the Navy just about the time Eddie's reputation began to rise. Eddie Gordon had a quiet reserved demeanor that attracted people. Men immediately liked him, and women stumbled over each other to serve him. As his pool game became sharper, his popularity soared. What used to be nickels and dimes turned into tens and twenties. Eddie would not let any of this newfound successes go to his head. He remained humble, and continued to work on his game. He also began to understand the other side of the coin.

Pool shooting is a very skillful game that requires dedication and determination. It's hard to become a great pool shooter without inflating your ego. Therefore, pool halls were filled with big egos and big pocketbooks. Eddie learned how to alleviate these great shooters of their pocketbooks, without destroying their fragile, inflated egos. It was a science he mastered that would keep a guy trying to beat you, until he was broke. That same cat would come back next week, and try again. Some guys would beat a person and talk so much trash, it destroyed the man's ego. Eddie would whip a guy in such a masterful way, he made the loser *feel good*. As his reputation took on a new level, so did the competition. Guys began to seek out Dan and the stakes grew larger.

This became apparently so at Miss Bee's Pool Room in North Philadelphia, as Dan sat around chatting with a few females, when the door swung open. A medium build man that looks about 40 years old came in, and the way everyone's heads turned, he was no stranger. The only person in the pool hall that seemed to not know Ted Lattimore, was Dan. He didn't pay the cat any immediate attention, until he realized the guy was looking directly at him, and started walking in his direction. Dan was a pretty good judge of people, and this guy did not appear to have any malicious intent, but because he did not know him, he kept an eye on him anyway. Dan continued to listen to the females' conversation, but now his attention was on the gentleman with a pool cue case in his hands.

"You English Dan", the man said in a baritone voice. That was the first time Dan had heard that term and for a split second it made him smile. "Yeah I'm Dan, who do I owe the pleasure?" "My name is Lattimore; they tell me you shoot a pretty good game." Dan just nodded his head and replied "I do all right", as Dan looked the man over. He noticed he was wearing a pair of cordovan colored penny loafers, which eliminated *hustler*, because most cats wore *Stacy Adams Wing Tips* or *Comforts*. Still Dan wondered about his intent. "What can I do for my friend?" Dan asked. Ted Lattimore bluntly replied "100 a game, straight pool!" "A man of very few words" quipped Dan, as he assessed how much money he had. He had about $580, which was good for five games. Dan never saw this man shoot, however he learned never to underestimate your opponent. "Let's do it", Dan shot back.

Straight pool is one of many pool games. In straight pool, players take turns trying to knock any of the 15 balls in the pocket until 1 ball is left. The pocketed 14 balls are racked, and the game continues until a player reaches 50 or 100 points. Another game is *8 Ball*, where players shoot at the *low* solid color balls or the *high* stripped colored balls. After the 7 balls are pocketed, the player that knocks in the 8 ball wins. *9 Ball* is played with just 9 balls numbered 1 through 9. Each player must knock the balls in according to their numerical order until the 9 ball is pocketed.

English Dan played them all, but he preferred to play *straight pool*. *8-Ball* and *9-Ball* are shorter games, however, *Straight Pool* is longer, and more enduring. It's like running a mile, and the others games are sprints. Dan watched guys fade away playing 3 or 4 games of *straight pool*. He could play for 8 hours straight, go home, take a shower, and play for 8 more. The fact that Ted Lattimore chose *straight pool* let Dan know he may be in for a good ole *dog fight*.

They both volleyed with the cue ball for the chance to shoot first. Ted Lattimore won, as Dan gestured to a young guy across the room. Sonny hung around the pool halls, and picked up tips racking and keeping score. Sonny racked the balls and reached up above the table with an old cue stick, and slid the ball counters to the left. The clacking sound of the counters made everyone in the pool hall, look in English Dan's direction. His reputation for a good, exciting match demanded attention, and apparently so did his opponent. As Dan chalked up the cue stick, he heard whispers that "Dan may have his hands full with Mr. Lattimore."

Ted calmly opened his cue case and began to screw his cue stick together. The cue stick was beautiful, and some people may have been impressed but English Dan was never excited about fancy sticks. Ted cracked the rack and 3 balls fell, he then moved with surgeon like precision, and pocketed the next 11. Sonny jumped up and racked the 14, and tallied the ball counters above the table. Ted knocked down the next rack even quicker. The score was 28 to 0 and Dan had not taken a shot. The crowd of about 15 whispered, and murmured in awe. English Dan now had reason to be impressed, and concerned. *Mr. Penny Loafers* dropped another 10 balls before he missed, then Dan went to work. He easily pocketed the last 4 balls, and Sonny tallied the counter and gave Dan a look of concern, as he racked the 14. English Dan never flinched, he knocked down the next rack and now the score was 38 to 18. Dan knew he could not afford to give his opponent another shot. Two balls into the rack, Dan missed a rather easy shot, and Ted ran the table and won the first game 50 to 20. English Dan reached into his pocket, and counted 5 twenties, and handed them to him and smiled. "Mr. Lattimore you shoot a pretty good game." Dan gestured to Sonny as he took off his sweater. "Let's do this again". Sonny racked the balls a little bit more deliberately, allowing Dan to compose himself. The crowd was even astonished by the precision of Ted Lattimore. They seldom saw Dan lose and they never saw a more worthy opponent.

The next game was closer 50 to 32, but Mr. Lattimore pocketed the five twenty dollar bills again. At that point, Dan realized he cannot let this cat shoot. In other words, once he misses, Dan must run the table. In other pool games such as *8 Ball* and *9 Ball*, there are certain *defensive* maneuvers you can employ, like *hiding* the cue ball or *blocking* the pocket. However, with *straight pool,* the only way you can slow down an offensive onslaught like Mr. Penny Loafers has displayed, is to keep him off the table. After pocketing the first 10 balls, he missed, and Dan took a sigh of relief. He slowly chalked his cue, and took a hard look at the table and dropped the remaining 4 balls. English Dan ran 2 ½ racks, and won 50 to 10. Sonny was visibly relieved as he racked the next game. The crowd of 15 had swelled to almost 30. It was as if someone was selling tickets, and Dan would not disappoint. He won the next 5 games, and for the first time, Mr. Lattimore was not that cool and collected anymore. English Dan made the cue ball dance to a tune that only he heard. The crowd oohed and aahed at the shots he made. The only thing Ted could do was watch. Now Sonny had a smile on his face as he racked, and Dan, as usual, kept his composure. He learned a while ago, never to express your feelings while shooting. Mr. Lattimore wasn't as cool, but he wasn't falling apart either. He had been in this situation many times. That's what gets his juices flowing, and that's why he seeks out the best players. "How bout we double the bet", he barked. Dan was up $400, along with the $580 he started with, this gave him enough for about 5 games. "Sure why not" as he smiled. Dan saw guys fall apart when the bets were increased, but he learned to keep an even keel, whether it was two dollars or two thousand.

Dan won the first game and then lost the next. After that it was all Dan, for the next 2 hours Dan won 10 games. Ted could not beat English Dan, and his ego would not allow him to admit it. As he counted out the 200 from the 10th game, Dan took the opportunity to get away from the table for a minute. He learned of the importance to unfix your eyes away from the table in these long matches. The green felt, and the balls sometimes would leave you in an optical trance. As he waded through the crowd to the Coca Cola machine across the room, Dan reached in his pocket for a nickel and bought a soda. The soda felt good going down, and it gave him a chance to reflect on what just occurred. When he arrived back at the table, he noticed what was once crisp twenty dollar bills, had diminished to fives and ones. Dan scooped up the two hundred dollars, and figured Lattimore was tapped out. He began to think about a hot shower, and changing his clothes, when Ted did something way out of his, once cool character. He reached into his pocket, and threw his car keys on the table and barked, "One more game, my car against one thousand dollars." The crowd went into a whispering frenzy. It caught English Dan completely by surprise. "Damn man, I don't want your car, how bout we call it a night." Ted shouted, "I don't give a damn about that car. I got a car lot with 200 cars on it, what I care about that goddamn car." Now Dan's memory cleared up, and he realized he was shooting Ted Lattimore, owner of Lattimore Oldsmobile, up on the boulevard. He had seen the name a hundred times, as he drove by his lot. Ted grew angrier, as he waited for Dan's answer and the once cordial, polite opponent turned into someone else. "Rack 'em Sonny", Dan fired back. Ted's frustration and fatigue had gotten the best of him. He couldn't make a shot. Dan won the match 50 to 4. As Mr. Lattimore began to unscrew his custom sculptured cue stick, Dan gave Sonny 60 dollars and another 40 dollar tip to Miss Bee, the owner. Ted was more embarrassed than ever as he walked out the door into the spring night. English Dan grabbed his sweater, and left also. He hastened his pace to try to catch up to his beaten opponent. Halfway down the block he shouted, "Ted give me a few ticks". The dejected Mr. Lattimore turned surprisingly. "Listen I don't want your car", Dan said, "I didn't want to show you up, but since you insisted I had to keep my reputation intact. How bout I bring your car to you in the morning and let me pick out something more of my taste. By the way it's a real nice car" as Dan nodded toward the shiny 1952 Oldsmobile parked a few feet away. How Ted managed to smile is a mystery, but he did, and shook Dan's hand and said, "Deal". English Dan learned a whole heap that night and he thinks he may have made a friend along the way.

The next morning Dan showed up at Lattimore Oldsmobile and picked out a nice 1952 Oldsmobile Rocket 88. The two of them had lunch and shared some of the fine pool shooting secrets. "Maybe we can go on the road sometime", Mr. Lattimore said. "I'm always looking for another challenge. I figure with you on my team we can't lose." They both laughed. "Incidentally Dan, I apologize for that outburst, that's not my style." "No offense taken my friend", as Dan walked over to his new car. "Not a bad night's work", Dan thought, as he drove towards his parent's apartment. He cleared close to three thousand dollars and a new car. If the pool hustling game was like it used to be, a night like this would be no big deal. But hustling pool was changing every day and beating Mr. Lattimore in front of that standing room only crowd, would make it even harder to get profitable matches.

Dan went into his parent's apartment, made a few phone calls and stashed a couple hundred dollars in a place he knew his mother would find. Nancy took care of all the bills. John Sr. didn't protest. It allowed him to go to work, come home and not be concerned with such matters. Dan thought about how lucky he was to have such good parents.

CHAPTER 2

Humble Beginnings

———

ONE WOULD THINK WHEN YOU looked at English Dan, with his fancy clothes, and smooth personae, that he was born, and raised in the big city. However, underneath all that shine and polish was a good old fashion country boy. In fact, he and his older brother, John, rarely mentioned this part of their life. A life that began hundreds of miles away.

Estill, pronounced "Estel", is located in the southernmost part of South Carolina. It was 52 miles north of the more popular Savannah Georgia and 93 miles west of Charleston. Established at the turn of 20th Century, Estill was over 70% black. Segregation and Jim Crow Laws made it *uncomfortable* for blacks to venture into white cities, therefore towns like Estill tend to remain heavily populated by the Negro. The total population was only a little over two thousand, which promoted a very familiar and close knit setting. Everyone knew each other by first name. Most of the families, both black and white were in this area since slavery back when the town was called "Lawnton". Their lineage and surnames were woven into the very fabric of this lumber, and farming community. The soil produced an above average grade of tobacco and cotton and the town prospered.

After the Civil War, the large plantation owners who were no longer the benefactors of *free labor* (slaves), were compelled to share their crops with the workers who tended them. Sharecropping became a way of life for blacks, and even for some white families. The financial agreements between the owners, and the workers were flawed, but an organized hard working family, could etch out a decent living.

The Perkin's Plantation, or farm as they were now called, was one of the largest in the area. It covered hundreds of acres of good farm land, and needed over twenty families to successfully reap its crop. Two of these families, the Speaks, and the Gordons worked side by side for many years. Nancy Speaks, one of the older siblings caught the eye of

John Gordon, and they soon married, and bore two sons, John Jr. and Eddie. For sharecroppers, a marriage and children meant more farm hands, and hopefully more revenue. Therefore, as soon as they were able to, John Jr. and Eddie worked the cotton, and white potato fields. Formal schooling was scheduled around the farm work, and sometimes, especially during harvest season, book learning took a *back seat* to the fields. It was a hard life, but it was a good simple life.

One beautiful Saturday morning right before the harvest season, John took the boys to the fields as he always did. There was not much work to do, just a few chores in preparation for the weeks to come. After the work was done, John loaded the buck board with his tools, and his sons, and headed to town. He wanted to treat the boys to some candy, and stop by the general store, and pick up a bottle of his favorite spirits. The horse was old, but still had a lot of life in his gait. It was given to John and Nancy a few years ago by Joe Givins, a neighbor, when he decided to say farewell to the farms, and took his family up north to Philadelphia. John was truly grateful for the horse, because it was one less debt he owed the Perkins.

The boys loved going to town, and sometimes their dad would allow them to hold the reins. John Jr., the elder by 3 years was obviously stronger and did a better job of controlling the horse but Eddie was unafraid of bringing the horse to a full gallop and this scared the begeebees out of his father. Eddie was not given the reins that often.

The town of Estill was small. There stood a tall water tower at one end of town, and a tiny train station nearby. The station was mostly for freight and mail, but you would sometimes see passengers waiting for the train that was only scheduled once a week. The brick and wood structured stores and shops separated by wide streets, covered about one square mile. At the other end of town, a row of horse stables, reminded any visitors that this was not the big fancy cities like Charleston, to the east, or Savannah, to the south. The Perkins Family owned the stables, and a half dozen of the other stores, and the Gilmores, another large land owner, owned quite a few also. Saturdays were usually the busiest day of the week as the town folk picked up necessities, and the farmers purchased supplies. The buckboards, pedestrians and the occasional automobile created a rather busy traffic pattern as the children played on the sidewalks.

There was an air of politeness and *southern hospitality* and for the most part the people both black and white, lived respectfully and with dignity. In spite of being located in the very heart of "Dixieland", the predominately black population, lived relatively free of hate, racism and segregation. However, everyone grew up knowing it was not that far away, like the potentially dangerous undercurrent beneath a seemingly calm sea.

John loved Saturdays. First because it signaled the end a long hard week, second it was a chance to call on his neighbors, shoot the breeze or go to town with his two sons. He gave the reins to John Jr., who steered the horse toward the big sign that read, Perkins General Store. As soon as he secured the horse, the anticipation and excitement overwhelmed the two boys, and they leaped off the buckboard. Their father then reached in his pocket, and gave them 10 cents each. They burst into the store and headed straight for the candy counter, as John Sr. methodically, and slowly trailed. Watching their enthusiasm brought a broad smile to his face, as he entered the store and headed for the liquor section. The boys quickly made their choices, left the store, jumped on the buckboard, and immediately began to enjoy their bag of treats. John was not in a hurry. He looked around the store, chatted with the clerk for a few minutes then purchased a pint of corn whiskey.

Upon leaving the store, the rays of the afternoon sun gave John Gordon a warm feeling inside. He glanced in the direction of his two sons, and then slipped into an alley way and took a small sip from his bottle. As he stepped back onto the busy street, he pondered how they could enjoy the rest of the afternoon. However, fate decided to interfere, and that ever so fragile state of being called happiness, was shattered. "Hey Nigger!" This huge 250lb white man about 25 feet away from John Gordon called. It caught the attention of the crowd nearby, but more importantly it startled Eddie and his brother. They heard the white men use that term before, but never with fierce intent. When John looked up, he saw Bobby Lee Gilmore coming in his direction.

Robert Lee Gilmore, named after the famous Civil War General, Robert E. Lee, was the grandson of the aging Clarence Gilmore, the patriarch of the Gilmore family. Bobby Lee was nothing more than a big bully but in his mind, he was the preserver of the *good ole days*. His job description was simple, "keep the coloreds in their place". Everyone in Estill knew him, and for the most part, everyone stayed out of his way. He was the face of that *undercurrent* running beneath the calm sea. "You heard me Nigger, you know it's against the law for you Niggers to drink on the street". He made it sound as if the law pertained to Niggers only. "I wasn't on the street," John insisted, "and why is this any of your business anyway." Bobby Lee was not used to people standing their ground, so this response caught him by surprise. The two boys watched intently. They didn't know much about Bobby Lee, but they knew their father, and they knew he was not going to back down. John did not wish this to go any further, and turned to walk away. Bobby lunged at him and tried to take the bottle out of his hands. John stepped back to avoid him, and calmly placed the bottle on the ground out of harm's way. This made Bobby Lee angrier, and he lunged once again. This time John simply leaned back just enough to get out his reach, and threw a perfect left hook to Bobby Lee's jaw. The punch made a bone cracking sound and before he could react, John hit him with another crushing left hook to the temple, followed by a right cross to the bridge of his nose. Bobby crumbled to the street like a sack of potatoes. John picked up his bottle, and walked away. The crowd stood there gawking, while some of them found a reason to smile at the sight of Bobby Lee knocked out cold, in the middle of the street. The boys may have been unsure what to do up to that point, but they knew it was time to go. Eddie snatched the reins, turned the buckboard around, and their father was barely aboard, when he slapped the horse with the reins, and took off. After about a mile outside of town, John collected himself, and took the reins from Eddie and rode home.

Nancy stood in the kitchen area of their 2 room sharecroppers hut. On the wood burning stove were two steaming hot pots. Beef stew was tonight's meal, and the pot roast was Sunday's dinner. As she turned the roast over to cook evenly, the boys burst through the door with their father not far behind. The sight of her boys brought a smile to her face and she embraced them. They began to tell her of their day in town. Still very excited by their experience, she could barely understand what they were saying. Eddie was not making much sense at all, then John Jr. took over the conversation, and now the story became clearer. Nancy's entire demeanor changed as she listened. Then without hesitation, she went to the bedroom, packed an overnight bag with her husband's clothes. She reached behind the bed into an old jar, and removed some of the cash. When she returned to the front room, John Sr. was peeping in the pots. When he turned around, and saw the overnight bag, that was the moment when reality set in.

Nancy wrote down a few addresses on a piece of a paper, then she walked over to her husband gave him a hug and said, "John honey you gotta go." John Gordon wanted to protest, but he knew she was right. He hugged his boys and left. Twenty minutes later there was a loud banging at the door. Nancy braced herself, and opened the door. A half dozen white men pushed their way into the house. Nancy grabbed her two sons. "Where is that damn husband of yours?" Before she could answer, two more men came in, one was Bobby Lee Gilmore. He was swollen and bruised. The other man she didn't know, however in his hands was a thick hangman's noose. He grabbed Nancy, and shook the noose in her face. "You tell that Nigger husband of yours, this is waiting for him when he returns."

The horse and buckboard would have provided a faster departure, but John figured finances would get a little tight in his absence. Nancy could fetch a nice price for the old nag. On the slip of paper his wife handed him, were a list of addresses. On that list were a small network of neighbors and relatives. Shortly after the Civil War, lynches rose dramatically. Now that Negroes were no longer property, and the whites were not benefactors of their *free labor*, killing and hanging them became a common occurrence. Records show that between 1870 and 1920, close to 5000 blacks were lynched. The motives for these atrocities would range from eyeballing and whistling at a white woman, to striking a white man, as was the case for John Gordon.

Communities across the South began to create a secret chain of *safe houses* to help facilitate a timely escape. In most cases, these routes to safety were successful. However, when the lynch mobs were sanctioned, and supported by the local law enforcement, informers could bring about a ghastly fate for the *underground railroad traveler.*

The first name on the list was his neighbor, Ezekiel Washington. His house was only a mile away. Walking at a rapid pace allowed him to arrive right around the same time Bobby Lee Gilmore and his pals pushed their way pass his wife, and two sons.

Thelma, Ezekiel's wife opened the door. Upon seeing John's overnight bag, Thelma immediately knew the reason for her neighbor's visit. Her husband had not returned from his Saturday field chores yet. Without speaking a word, she motioned to John to sit down and have supper with her 2 sons and 2 daughters. John politely obliged, and went through the back door to the well to wash his hands. When Zeke, as everyone called him, pushed through the front door, he was delighted to see his neighbor, but he knew this was not a social call.

After a quiet dinner, the two of them went into the backyard. John told him of his ordeal in town. Zeke didn't respond, he simply patted John on the back in a comforting manner. They both knew the next part of this journey would be the most important, and also the most dangerous. Zeke prepared his horse and buckboard, as Thelma packed them some essentials. The next house was the Wilsons, and it was 3 hours away. Fortunately, this leg of the trip went without incident. The moonlit sky provided just enough light for them to reach their destiny without detection. Zeke returned home well past midnight. He was exhausted, but he would do it all over again tomorrow if necessary. The thought of seeing one of his neighbors or relatives, hanging from a tree, was more than enough motive.

John rested in the Wilson's barn and was aroused at daybreak by Willie Wilson's oldest son, Luke. He pointed to the family's old car, and drove John to the bus station. The bus would take John Gordon into the next county, out of harm's way, where he would catch a train into Philadelphia. The last name and address on the list, was Joe Givins, his friend and former neighbor. He made room in his home for John, and helped him get a job at the factory where he worked. In a little less than 2 months, John Gordon, sent for his wife and 2 sons. It didn't take long for Nancy and her 2 sons to get used to the big city life. Her beloved husband embraced his new surroundings, but he often wondered what his life would have been, if fate had not crossed his path on that beautiful Saturday afternoon in Estill South Carolina.

CHAPTER 3

A Shark in Different Waters

THE PECULIAR THING ABOUT HUSTLING pool, is you meet all types of people. When shooting pool was at its height in the late 1940's and early 1950's, it produced a large variety of pool hustlers. There were regular cats who worked during the day and hustled at night. You're not going to get any high wages out of that bunch, but they were still formidable opponents. Then you had street hustlers, such as number writers, con men and drug dealers. The wages were larger, but so was the bullshit you had to endure. Last, you had your professional types, doctors, lawyers and business men like Ted Lattimore. The one thing they all had in common was their pool shooting egos were always greater than their pool shooting abilities. This is how genuine pool hustlers like English Dan made a living. The phrase *pool shark* could not be more descriptive of their lifestyle. A shark is always moving, hunting for smaller fish, different waters. It was now time for Dan to seek out new territory. The North Philly pool halls became harder and harder to earn in. English Dan heard about a popular spot down South Philly owned by a cat named Chick Davis. Maybe it's time he paid Mr. Davis a visit.

Dan counted out $500, that's all he ever carried into a pool hall. He figured if he can't beat you with $500, he can't beat you. Also, if he were to be robbed, $500 is all they would get. He stashed the rest in a hole in the wall in his bedroom. He could have taken it over to an older female's house, he saw from time to time but that level of trust had not been achieved yet. Mom and Pop was a *sure bet*.

Philadelphia is a city full of neighborhoods. The people in these neighborhoods usually stayed close to their boundaries. South Philly cats seldom ventured north and North Philly were very comfortable on the north side of City Hall. Dan was different; he went all over the city even as a youth. He knew how to navigate areas and he also knew how to *hold his hands*, if necessary.

It was early spring and the weather was beautiful. Dan didn't have many vices but if you can call immaculate dressing a vice, then he was guilty of that. Feeling pretty good about himself, he put on one of his finest outfits with a pair of chocolate brown presidents. He loved the East River Drive and pointed his car in that direction as the soulful sound of Nat King Cole came across the radio.

At first sight, Dan found the Rodman Street Pool Hall un-impressing, but as he descended in the *grotto style* entrance, he began to get excited. It should be mentioned that English Dan got excited any time he stepped into a pool hall. The joint was almost empty, except for a couple of chicks in the corner conversing. It was only 3 in the afternoon, and that's early for a pool hall. Dan's impeccable attire immediately attracted the two females. Dan assessed that they were easy on the eyes also. The one named Charlotte was the talkative one and the quiet listener was Amy. He later learned they were the Burnett sisters. Two of the four sisters from one of those famous South Philly families headed by a matriarch, named Tuesday. Everyone in South Philly knew Ms. Tuesday and Ms. Tuesday knew everyone in South Philly. Her family of 3 sons and 4 daughters was not the benefactors of wealth and crime like the Andersons. However, their name rang in all 4 corners of South Philly.

Dan leased a rack of balls from a fair-skinned cat behind the counter and began to do a few *trick shots*. The Burnett sisters were drawn to the table, and Dan turned up the entertainment and the charm. English Dan was a pool hustler to the core. He didn't go in for those circus acts, but he was just killing time, besides he had a captive audience. The two Burnett sisters were amazed, and amused be the pool shooting talent of this smooth well-dressed stranger. "I'm Charlotte, this is my sister Amy, never seen you around these parts before," she confidently implied. At first Dan didn't respond at all. He was taken by surprise at her straight forwardness. Then he smiled and said, "I'm Dan, and that's because I'm not from around these parts", he said with a touch of cynicism. Her sister, Amy, wanted to disappear. She was embarrassed by her sister's boldness, but also wanted to benefit from her boldness and find out more about this sharp fella named Dan. Charlotte continued her persistence as Dan engaged in a little small talk with the *chatty* one, but was now visually focused on the *quiet one*.

It was after 5pm now, and people began to come into the pool hall. Dan stopped doing the *trick shots* because he did not want to scare off any potential bettors. However, at the request of Amy, Dan promised to show her one more shot. He lined up the balls and performed the shot, but now he had a larger audience. A well-dressed cat in his mid-twenties intervened. "Bet you can't do that when money on the table", interjected the newcomer. Dan thought to himself, here we go again. "Just playing around with the ladies my friend", Dan said. "You haven't answered my question!" the newcomer replied. "Well, what kind of money are we talking about and what kind of game", Dan shot back. "Nine Ball, fifty a game Willie cracked." It seemed to Dan he was trying to impress Amy and Charlotte, which implied that he wasn't a *genuine* pool hustler. "I'm Dan, let's do it!" it was the quickest 9-Ball game Dan had ever shot. Dan thought, "Either this cat is trying to hustle me or he just can't shoot to save his life." When the cat excused himself and went to the bathroom, Dan took the opportunity to find out more about Willie. "Charlotte, you know this guy?" "Yeah, he works for P.J., you know the Andersons", she said as if everyone should know that. "They control most of the numbers." said Charlotte. "I heard they also are in the dope business," Amy interceded. It pleasured Dan to hear any words from Amy. However, this information was helpful, especially coming from her. The insightful news was informative, but it still didn't tell Dan if this guy could shoot pool or not, and as he approached the table, Dan said to himself, "we will certainly find out." When Willie lost the sixth game, he began to get loud and boisterous and when he began to curse, it caught the attention of the fair skinned man behind the counter.

"This motherfucker hustled me. That was the fastest three hundred dollars I ever lost." retorted Willie. "Y'all gonna let this slick motherfucker get away with this?" "Showing off for the ladies again Willie?" the fair skinned man said. "Don't come over fucking with me while I am losing my money Chick, and who is this sucker anyway", pointing to Dan. "I watched the whole thing, you bet, you lost, you pay. You know my rules around here Willie, besides you know you can't shoot pool, I don't know why you even try. You ain't P.J." Chick said with a chuckle. Apparently everyone in the hall knew this character, because no one was aroused by his antics. Charlotte and Amy were in the corner snickering as he continued his side-show. "Willie, if you can't control yourself, you got to go", Chick demanded. Dan had stepped back a little, but kept the pool cue stick in his hand just in case this asshole wants to take it any further. "I'm sorry, my name is Chick Davis we run a respectable place around here." "I'm Dan, first time here. I heard you ran one of the best pool halls this side of City Hall." "You from North Philly," Chick said with delight. You English Dan?" Dan just nodded. "I heard good things about you Dan. Good news travels fast in these halls," Chick said with an air of respect. The place was filling up pretty good and all of the tables were used except the one covered table in the center of the room. "I notice you keep that table covered," inquired Dan. "We keep that one in the mothballs for that special game. The felt is always in tip top shape, I'm able to turn up the lights over the top and the wood is always polished," Chick said proudly. "From what I heard about you Dan, I wouldn't be surprised if you were playing on my centerpiece one day." "You think too much of me Mr. Davis, I'm just a young country boy in the Big City." "I saw the way you pounced on Willie in those *9-Ball* games and you were still in first gear. This cat is not indicative of the crowd we attract. A top level hustler like you can do pretty well in my place, English Dan. I hope you pay us a visit more often." Dan was enjoying this conversation, when he realized that Willie was still standing at the table dumbfounded as if he were awaiting Dan's return. However, Dan learned a long time ago that combative opponents like Willie were bad news. So you just gonnna quit on me Mr. English Dan," he said with an overdose of sarcasm. "No my friend, I'm gonna go and partake of the company of these two lovely ladies, you tried so hard to impress". "Fuck them and fuck you," as he stormed out the door and up the steps. "Is he always like this?" Dan asked Charlotte. "Hell no, when P.J. is around he's quiet as a church mouse. That three hundred he lost was probably P.J.'s money." Dan pondered on that statement and departed, but not before he slipped Amy his home phone number. The night was still early and he could have gone back to North Philly in search of another game, but he had seen enough green felt over the last 2 days. He slowly drove towards the East River Drive and pointed his car in the direction of his female friend. He had not seen Violet in a few days and he could use a little rest and relaxation and a home cooked meal.

CHAPTER 4

The Birth of A Living Nightmare

THE HEROIN BUSINESS IN AMERICA with all of its destructive glory, started out in a very inconspicuous way. At the end of the 19th Century, the Chinese Immigrants were the backbone of the labor force used to build the American Railways. They brought with them an array of cultural icons unknown to the West. Opium smoking was not an unusual sight, after a hard day of laying tracks, or even herding cattle. In the early part of the 20th Century, heroin was manufactured from opium and the Chinese introduced it to the United States. It was initially used for medicinal purposes, however, when the United States Government placed it on its illegal contraband list, the Chinese Black Market became its sole purveyor. Heroin is highly addictive, and when it's in its purest form, it can be heavily diluted. These two factors would eventually attract the attention of the organized crime world. Once the heroin trade became *organized* in the late 1930's, it spread across the country with the same efficiency as the construction of the interstate highway system. When its deadly inventory traveled down the New Jersey Turnpike into the North Jersey cities, it left a trail of pain and destruction. When heroin was introduced to Philadelphia, Louie Appellini was its number one advocate. Many of the old mob associates were still leery on the ramifications of their new found enterprise, but the *young guns* were ready to take the risk for the lucrative financial return.

The one problem that faced the Mob was finding people at the street level to sell their wares. These people had to be trusted, with finances and the vow of silence. Louie Apples would go to the Andersons and tell Peter Sr. and his brothers of his new acquired business. Louie could have easily been aggressive and demanded that they cooperate, but he had a tremendous amount of respect for Peter Sr. When the father got the message to meet with Louie, he simply smiled. Peter Anderson Sr. was a very smart businessman long before he got in the bed with the mob. He made it his business to see situations long before they showed themselves. When the New York Mob started selling heroin, Peter was one of the first to know. He knew a few high ranking numbers bankers in Harlem, and they kept him informed on the current affairs. When New York started something, it was just a matter of time before it came to Philly. Peter also researched the legal, and environmental consequences of the heroin trade. His lawyers told them to be very cautious, and his conscience made him question his involvement in a destructive business that was targeted for Black People. Nonetheless, he agreed to meet with Louie, but first he and his brothers needed to sit down and formulate a plan of their own.

Peter Sr. was the oldest of Carl and Phillip Anderson. Their parents made a decent living from a grocery store at 12th & Lombard Streets in South Philly. Peter dropped out of school at the age of 15 and proved to be a very astute businessman. By the time he reached 20, Peter turned the modest store into an expanded market, and with the help of his two brothers, created four more stores. His younger brothers had the utmost respect for Peter. However, they wondered how was he going to handle the Louie "Apples" situation?

"Listen fellas", Peter began, "Louie's gonna be here in about 3 hours, I need your undivided attention and all of your input on this matter." Phillip Anderson, the youngest brother, lit a cigarette and Carl walked over to the cabinet to fix a drink. Peter's house was beautiful, the numbers were good to the Andersons, and they were grateful. "We talked about this before, long before it came down the pike. We are number bankers, and none of us has ever seen the inside of a jail cell." The two younger brothers nodded with approval. "We grossed over a million dollars last year and probably will do better this year. Louie's people are very satisfied with our ability to earn. So therefore that makes this meeting about our strengths and we must make sure Louie knows that. Sure, we could refuse this offer, don't know how that would play out with Louie, but we knew there would be choices we don't agree with, when we bedded down with our *Meditterean Friends.*" Over the next three hours, Peter and his brothers carefully planned their strategy.

Louie Appellini was greeted with smiles and hugs from the Anderson Brothers. They all took notice that Louie brought his *brain trust lieutenant* with him. Paulie was a mathematical phenom. Whenever you saw him, that indicated numbers, deals, percentages, but whenever he brought his other lieutenant, Joe-Joe, his job was simple, planting fear. Peter had some imported Italian olives, fresh baked bread and a couple carafes of wine on the table. Louie loved olives, and he didn't hesitate to dive into the bowl, as Paulie presented the deal to the brothers. "You guys don't have to put up no bread", he said with a strong Italian accent. "We need you guys to setup distribution, and collections. We'll take care of packaging, and we even have a couple of *shysters* to handle any legal problems. We can make this happen for 40/60 breakdown of the profits". Louie reached for the loaf of bread and waited for a response from Peter. He knew Peter Sr. would not accept this deal because this proposal would lock him into the mob. This deal would have been great for an organization with minimum capital and did not care about the *mob attachment*. Those two factors did not describe the Andersons. "So Pete whatta yah think" mumbled Louie. "Lou you already know what I think" as he broke a tiny smile. "We are policy bankers, Lou we're not drug dealers.

Why would we disturb the beautiful relationship we have?" as he threw up his hands in bewilderment. "We can write and bank numbers for the next hundred years, but this drug thing has a shelf life. How long do you think this thing is gonna last before it comes tumbling down?" Louie just nodded in partial agreement. "However", Peter continued, "I know what this means to you and the only reason you came to me, was because of my ability to setup an operation like this." Peter directed his conversation towards his lieutenant. "This is what we can do Lou. You guys are getting your product for about $10,000 per pound." This made Louie sit up at full attention. "We'll buy 5 pounds at 20 grand a piece of the pure product with our own cash and give you an additional 10 percent of the profits on the back end. We should be able to work that off in 6 months, and then we'll do it once more. After the two deals, I will personally make sure you are connected with the right people to continue your operation, then me and my family are out. I'll tell my son and my nephew to get with Paulie to work out the figures." Peter looked at Louie without blinking and waited for a response. "That's a rough deal, Pete." Louie looked at Paulie for help. Louie was stunned by Peter Sr.'s in depth knowledge of the heroin trade, and also his insight of the Mob's financial dealings. "Whatta yah think Paulie", Lou asked his trusted mathematician. "Well, Lou 50 grand off the top and at least another 100 grand on the back. It's a good deal Boss." "One more thing", Peter intervened, "the numbers racket and this business shall never meet, in fact you and I never have to discuss this anymore." As Lou and Paulie gathered themselves to leave, Peter walked them to the door. As he opened the door he whispered in Lou's ear, "Consider that favor you did for me a few years ago paid in full."

"Listen Carl and Phillip, let's get one thing straight," Peter demanded of his brothers, "we are only going to do these 2 deals, it's a lot of money in that poison, but it's also a lot of jail time and aggravation. Carl your son and P.J. will handle the operation. I've got a guy in New York that's gonna come down and show them how to cut and package the product. Also never bring that stuff around our numbers houses." Carl and Phillip left the Gray's Ferry Avenue townhouse and Peter sat down and pondered on the ramifications of the meeting and that tiny smile resurfaced again, when he thought about the expression on Louie's face.

Carl's only son Matthew, was two years younger than P.J. but had the quiet resolve of a much older man. He wasn't as flashy as his cousin and didn't shoot pool in fact, he was an excellent chess player. It was no surprise that when their heroin business began to succeed, it was Matthew who took the lead position, and P.J. handled a lot of the actual street operations. Matthew listened intently to his father Carl and his Uncles Peter and Phillip about the dangers, and destructive environment that their business would create. He immediately did not like it; however, he ran the business with precision. P.J. on the other hand immediately was swept away by the attention, and power it brought. A few months into the new business, Matthew longed for the carefree daily operations of the numbers racket. Whereas, P.J. literally threw himself into the new business, and relished on the drama and excitement that accompanied it. One of the most important factors that were required of such a dangerous business was a good sense of judgment when selecting the people, you choose to trust. P.J. had problems with that.

In a very lucrative operation as the drug business, you need at least three trusted lieutenants. Their job would be to distribute and to collect. P.J.

was instructed to choose no one affiliated with the numbers racket so he reached out to a few cats he grew up with. Harry T was perfect. He was shrewd, had a lot of respect on the street and was very trustworthy with cash. Then there was Dave, he was an excellent business man but had a disturbing weakness for the games of chance. His third choice was Willie. They were best friends since grade school, and that may have been his only qualifying factor. Willie loved to chase the females and he also was reckless gambler, not to mention a very bad pool shooter. The first deal went as planned.

Just when the Andersons were halfway out of the drug business, P.J. committed a treacherous act that would send shock waves through South Philly and no one would look at P.J. the same way including his father. It was a typical spring Saturday morning in South Philly. The neighborhood was alive with horse drawn hucksters selling their wares. People were sweeping their white alabaster front steps. The Italian Market at 9th and Christian Street was bustling with shoppers and merchants. You could smell the hot roast beef, and roast pork from the tiny luncheonettes, as the huge jars of colorful hot peppers decorated their counters. No one loved a hot roast beef sandwich more than Dave, and every Saturday after a hard Friday night of collections and distributing, he found solace in the sandwich, and a little conversation on the corner with the fellas. As he emerged from the luncheonette with his roast beef sandwich. He saw a few of his buddies on the corner. He turned toward them and made a friendly gesture, but he did not see the shadowy figure coming behind him. Before he could react, the shadowy figure swung the baseball bat, and crushed the right side of his knee joint. The cracking sound of crumbling bones got the attention of the men across the street, but before anyone could react, the attacker broke the other leg with two more devastating blows. The excruciating pain sent Dave's entire body into shock, so much that he could not even muster a scream. He made a grunting sound as he tried to gather his senses, and as his blurring eyes began to clear, he saw P.J. calmly walking away with the bat on his shoulder.

The once cool and likeable pool shooter, had transformed into someone no one knew. It was said that Dave, due to his gambling came up short on the collections, one too many times, and a few harsh words were exchanged. Dave was an excellent hustler and always paid what he owed and this treacherous act on P.J.'s childhood friend was unnecessary. Some say that P.J. changed ever since he started hanging out with Louie Apple's psychopathic lieutenant, Joe-Joe. Peter Anderson Sr. was livid. He knew dumping ten pounds of poison on the community he loved, would have consequences. However, he never thought that repaying the favor that protected his son from the dangers of war, would one day unravel the fabric of his beloved family, he worked so hard to hold together. Peter Sr. was deeply saddened by the doctor's report. It said that Dave, the young man who once ran and played in his backyard as a child may never walk again.

CHAPTER 5

The Set-Up

———

IT WAS NEARLY A MONTH since Dan beat Willie, P.J.'s lieutenant out of three hundred dollars at Chick's Pool hall. He yearned to return, and see what other fish he could swallow up, but lately his attention was on another South Philadelphian. He and the quiet Burnett sister, Amy had a few nice phone conversations since then. They talked about everything. He was amazed and impressed by her level of intelligence. She could hold a conversation about anything, world events, historic events and such. She told him of the horrible story about P.J. and his lieutenant, David. The story puzzled Dan because from all of the things he heard about P.J., he assumed he was a cool cat. They agreed to go on a date, so he put on some of his finest duds and polished his 1952 Oldsmobile, and headed down Broad Street to South Philly. Halfway down Broad Street he realized they never agreed on a time, so he stopped at a telephone booth and called. The operator told him that the *party line* was being used and he should try back later. Dan decided to proceed anyway.

South Philadelphia and Center City are where the original inhabitants of Philadelphia lived and subsequently it was where the first blacks of the city resided and planted their roots. Tuesday Burnett was born in 1902 in Chester Pennsylvania, a city 20 miles southwest of Philly. She moved to South Philly as a child and she never left. Fifty years and three major wars later, Tuesday was like a rock, a polished precious gem tempered by time, defined by her family and very comfortable being "Ms. Tuesday". Dan had never met Amy's mother, but he had no doubt the small stately woman standing outside the courtyard style row houses on Fitzwater Street near 12th Street was Ms. Tuesday. "Ma'am is Amy at home?" Dan asked nervously. "And who may I ask is calling son." "I'm Dan, she is expecting me." Ms. Tuesday looked him up and down, looked at the shiny car and pointing toward the courtyard entrance. "She's in the rear house 1238." Dan had braced himself for some sort of confrontation with the popular Ms.

Tuesday, but when nothing happened, he found himself still standing there for a few seconds, until she broke a small smile and said "she's waiting for you." Dan scurried into the courtyard and gazed at the colonial style architecture. This section of South Philadelphia was vintage and these particular row houses had to have been at least 150 years old or more. The front of the courtyard was flanked by two small houses connected by a brick archway and the two rear houses existed on the opposite side of the rear yard. Dan felt a special feeling of family in the tiny courtyard, and it had Ms. Tuesday's fingerprints all over it. Amy's slender frame appeared at the front door and for a split second Dan did not recognize her. The woman he remembers at the pool hall was a teenager with high school looks. The female he saw in the doorway, was a beautiful statuesque woman.

They decided to just go for a ride through the park. Dan did not drink, and Amy did not go out that often, so a nice slow ride around the West and East River Drives was perfect. They stopped, and chatted and Amy asked Dan about his ambitions and goals. "I'm embarrassed to say I never gave it much thought" Dan reveals. He then realizes that he also never indulged in a serious relationship that warrants such dialogue. "Amy, right now I'm a pool hustler, and damn good at it, I would like to reserve the right to finish the answer to your question at another time." "No problem Eddie, you take all the time you need." Hearing her use his birth name brought a sense of reality, to the moment and made Dan smile. She was very special.

Pool like any other skill needs repetitious practice. While keeping the company of the beautiful Ms. Amy Burnett was good for Dan's heart, it was not helping his pool game. The only way a *pool shark* stays on top of his game is to stay in the water. To stay competitive, you must compete regardless of how good you were yesterday, and you are only as good as the opponents you beat today. At the Ridge and Colombia Avenue pool hall, Dan lost $250.00 to a mediocre player. Dan was rusty, and it left a bad taste in his mouth. The North Philly halls were gradually dying out. It was getting harder every day to get a decent game. "It's time to pay Mr. Chick Davis another visit" Dan said to himself.

It was a beautiful Friday evening, so Dan figured it might be a nice idea to invite Amy and Charlotte out. "We'll get a bite to eat and then we'll go to

Chick's, I need the action" Dan told Amy over the phone. When Dan pulled up to the courtyard, Amy and Charlotte were waiting outside. Ms. Tuesday's nest was almost empty. The three eldest, Elizabeth, George and Leon were long gone and Charlotte was engaged to be married. That left Amy, and the two teenagers, Eddie and Marion. Ms. Tuesday was standing on the corner chatting with some neighbors. She waved as they drove by. "I think she likes me" Dan said with an air of confidence. When the two daughters didn't respond, his confidence evaporated into the spring night air. Amy and Charlotte enjoyed the steak sandwiches, but Dan's taste buds were not working. He was merely going through the motions of enjoying the meal, and their company. English Dan had one thing on his mind.

Broad and South was alive with activity. Every time the door at Peps Musical Bar opened, you could hear the blaring sound of the saxophone. However, Dan didn't hear anything. He walked past the crowd, and slipped down Rodman Street. Amy and Charlotte were taking their time conversing with people along the way. The pool hall was packed. Dan paused and looked around as he saw Chick Davis behind the counter. He nodded in his direction. Chick waved him over. "I'm glad to see you again, the action is on the left side of the room" he whispered. Trying not to point, Chick nodded in the direction of two well-dressed cats playing *9-Ball*. "The tall one is Cool Breeze, the other one I don't know, but they came here with one thing in mind, just figured you'd like to know that", he said with a smile. Dan wandered over to their table to take a closer look.

The tall cat, Cool Breeze was having his way with the shorter guy. Dan never had any doubt in his pool skills, so whoever the opponent was he approached them all the same. But lately his pool game was a little suspect, so he looked to see if he could spot any weaknesses in Cool Breeze's game. After a few games, Dan shook his head and thought "if there are any I don't see them". The shorter guy was almost tapped out. You could tell by his facial expression as he forked over the fifty-dollar pay-off. At a table right across from them, Dan noticed something he had not seen in a while. There was an older guy with a receding hairline, *stake horsing* a young cat about 18 years old. Stake horsing is when the cat with the dough, bets on the shooter and they usually agree on a 40/60 split. In most cases, the shooter is usually a hotshot kid with extraordinary skills, and the broker usually has deep pockets. Dan thought to himself, "If I can rattle this kid, maybe I could take them for a few bucks". Dan also thought there was a reason Chick didn't point me in this direction. Let's see how good this kid is.

Dan found out the kid's name was Ruben and his backer was an old hustler name Leon. They were playing *9-Ball* for fifty bucks a game. Ruben was very good, perhaps better than Cool Breeze at the other table. Everything that Dan learned over the last 4 or 5 years, says stay away from this buzz saw, but his competitiveness drew him closer to the table. Ruben controlled the cue ball and made it look real easy. Dan watched as he knocked off 3 cats out of a total of four hundred and fifty dollars. They probably all thought what Dan thought, they could rattle the youngster and get into the deep pockets of Leon. Dan was about to walk away when Leon said, "You want some of this English Dan?" The sarcastic tone did exactly what it was designed to do. Dan grabbed a cue stick, never mind how this cat knew his name. "Let's raise the stakes $100.00 a game my friend", Dan said. Leon hesitated for a second and then said, "Bet". Dan raised the stakes to see if it would put a little more pressure on the kid and it worked. He didn't drop any balls on the break and Dan ran the table. "You gotta be careful what you ask for Mister you seem to know me but what's your name?" "Leon", he barked with a touch of anger as he gave Dan the one hundred dollars." Dan heated up the next game. He dropped the 9 ball on the break winning the game instantly. Ruben settled down and won the third game, but Dan was stellar, he won the next 6 games. Amy and Charlotte had made their way through the crowd that was now surrounding their table. Dan cut a small smile at Amy as he chalked up his cue stick for the 10th game. Ruben was a little better in this game, but stares and disappointing sounds coming from his backer, disturbed Ruben and Dan won again. Stake horsing is a lot like being in the corner of a young prize fighter. When your star finally gets a real test, you don't let him get his brains knocked out so you take him out and save him to fight another day. However, you want that test to be a learning experience, so Leon decided on one more game. He even pulled his young prospect over, and whispered a few pointers to him. Just as Dan broke, the crowd's attention was drawn to the entrance and the welcoming shouts of "P.J., P.J.!!!"

P.J. Anderson was still the *prince* of this part of town, even though his recent behavior made people whisper a lot more. The Anderson Family employed many people in South Philly and their reputation was etched in stone. For a few minutes, everyone's attention was on P.J. Even Ruben paused from the game, and looked in the direction of the *heralded one*. Seeing this, Dan took a moment to check him out also. He was well-dressed, and had a certain arrogant, but likeable air about him. His hair was processed but very professionally groomed. Chick came from behind his counter, and personally greeted P.J. and they shook hands and hugged. Dan was about to return to his game, when he noticed coming behind P.J. were two chicks and Willie, the sore losing pool shooter. "This night just got more interesting", Dan whispered to himself. "Ruben it's your shot." No balls fell when Dan broke, so Ruben knocked down the one, the two and missed on the three. Dan pocketed the three ball but the four ball was blocked by the eight. As Dan paused to calculate the next move, P.J. spotted Leon and walked toward him. "Leon, who are you staking, what young stud are you pimping now he said with a laugh." "P.J. watch your mouth you know I invest in only the finest thoroughbreds. Don't forget I got you started", as they hugged. Leon was right, he stakehorsed P.J. when he was a hotshot teenage star.

"Ruben this is Mr. P.J." "Hello Mr. P.J.", Ruben said in a humble tone. "He treating you right son?" P.J. replied. "Yeah we were doing alright until we ran into this English Dan cat, Leon said sarcastically. When Willie heard the name English Dan, he turned around and shouted "P.J. that's that motherfucka I was telling you about. He hustled me out of $300.00." Dan retuned his focus to the game and shouted "4 ball corner right." Dan cocked his cue stick in an upright position and made a chopping swipe at the cue ball, causing the ball to go around the eight ball and knock the four ball in the corner. The crowd went crazy. He ran the rest of the table with relative ease. In a matter of a few minutes, the focus was no longer on South Philly's finest but on the smooth, dapper stranger from North Philly. As Dan goes to shake Ruben's hand, he pats Leon on the shoulder and says "good game." P.J. was impressed and a little envious of the slender stranger. "How much were y'all playing for Leon?" "I let this sucka talk me into upping the bet to one hundred a game." Dan waved Chick over to the table and tipped him fifty bucks. "So Chick when you starting letting these North Philly cats in?" P.J. implied. Chick just smiled because he saw where this was going. "Alright Mr. English Dan since you so good, how bout we get Chick to uncover the center table and we go at it for let's see, a thousand a game", P.J. boasted. The crowd gasped in awe of such numbers. At that point P.J. pulled a huge wad of money from his pockets when one of the girls they brought in, tugged him on the arm and said in a complaining voice, "I thought we supposed to be going out tonite, P.J." Dan replied, "I tell you what Mr. Anderson whenever you find time, you let me know, but in the meanwhile, why don't you give your partner Willie a few dollars and let me beat up on him." The whole place laughed including P.J. "Fuck you Dan and fuck all y'all" as he grabbed his date, and started heading for the exit. "Alright Mr. Hotshot, as you can see I'm a very busy man, I ain't got the time to shoot you all night for this money so, how 'bout we do this next Friday right here at 8 o'clock for five g's!" The place went deafly silent. Everyone was waiting on Dan's answer especially Amy. She said to herself, "I know damn well Eddie is not going to play him for no five thousand dollars." But before she could complete that thought, Dan blurted "I'll be there", and for a split second he felt like he was duped into this wager. But that feeling went away as quick as it came and Dan added, "Chick dust off the center table." "Will do, Dan, will do!" The crowd murmured as the other tables tried to refocus on their games, but everyone in that pool hall was thinking about next Friday's five-thousand-dollar pool match.

As Dan, Amy and Charlotte walked to the car, there was an eerie silence between them caused by deep contemplation. Charlotte was thinking of how she was going to tell her mother about this crazy wager. Amy was trying to find a few choice words for Mr. Eddie Gordon, and Dan was trying to calm himself down and take an inventory as to what just took place and equally as important an inventory of his cash stashed at his mother's apartment. "Eddie Gordon it's 1952, do you know what five thousand dollars can buy or how long it takes the average worker to earn five thousand dollars", Amy spouted breaking the silence. Dan did not reply. He knew how long it took him to earn that five thousand dollars and right now that's all that mattered. Amy was right again and her level of reality and responsibility always kept Dan's feet on the ground. Yes, it is

1952 and a quart of milk is 25¢, and you can rent a nice apartment for about $60.00 a month, and the average cat takes down about $40 a week for forty hours of work, but P.J. and English Dan were not your average cats.

CHAPTER 6

The Match

———

ENGLISH DAN LOVED THE PHILADELPHIA night life, the pool halls and all of the excitement that came with it. However, he also found the mornings just as attractive. Dan was born down South, but he spent most of his young life in North Philadelphia. After the Depression, North Philadelphia became one of the country's most productive industrial areas and Dan was living right in the center of it. At the crack of dawn, North Philly's streets filled up with workers on their way to the multitude of factories and shops along Lehigh and Allegheny Avenues. Some of the country's most productive garment makers were nestled in the heart of North Philadelphia. Botany 500 was located at Broad Street and Lehigh Avenue and Empire Sportswear at 22nd Street and Lehigh Avenue. The Heppenstall Steel Mill on Wissahickon

Avenue was busy as ever, as was the Budd Plant down the street on Hunting Park Avenue. All of this employment translated into vibrant neighborhoods, and very successful local businesses. Nonetheless, Dan liked to be in the company of the working folk. It gave him a sense of balance between his lifestyle and theirs. So every morning, Dan would frequent one of the many popular breakfast spots and rub elbows with the nine to fivers. Today, he chose Broad Street and Susquehanna Avenue, because afterwards he needed to get a few quality pool games under his belt in preparation for Friday's big match. Sugarfoot's Pool Hall was right down the street and in this particular hall; you could still find decent competition.

The waitress asked for Dan's order but for a moment, he did not hear her because he was pondering the gradual disappearance of the game he loved so much. The thought saddened him, but he reflected on Amy's question about his life's direction, and he smiled thinking one day he too, will be one of these working stiffs. Dan was only twenty-two, however he knew he could not hustle pool forever. He decided to order something different. "May I have an order of corn beef hash and two sunny side up eggs with toast"? The waitress did not verbally respond she wrote the order down and quietly walked away. The restaurant was a little crowded and Dan spotted some of his regular buddies, but he was not in the mood for much banter, and chose to quietly eat his breakfast. He tipped the waitress, and headed for the door. He was itching to get a pool cue in his hand, because as much as he tried not to think about this upcoming match he found it impossible.

Sugarfoot leased the pool hall from a Jew named Josh Redman. In the beginning, he did rather well, but since the decline of pool shooters, Sugarfoot had to write numbers in the back room to make up the difference. So every morning Sugarfoot had to get up no later than 6AM in the morning, clean up the pool hall, and clear his schedule because all of his numbers had to be turned in before 1PM. As Dan slowly pulled up to the curb, Sugarfoot was sweeping the front pavement, and listening to these two other cats having a heated debate. "I'm telling you the 2nd Negro Baseball player that was chosen by the major leagues, was Satchel Paige," shouted Leroy. "Nigger you must be out of your mind; Satchel didn't get drafted for another year. Jackie Robinson went in 1947, Paige in 1948. Larry Dolby was the second black player chosen," the older gentleman insisted.

Dan found this very interesting because he didn't follow baseball that closely, so he too was curious about who was second. It's been 5 years since the Dodgers chose Jackie, and the Negro League went into immediate decline. There were still a few good players left in the Negro League but it was only just a matter of time. "How much you got to lose", Leroy shouted back. "Scotty is right Leroy", intervened Sugarfoot. "I'm gonna save your black ass some money, it was Larry Dolby, drafted by the Cleveland Indians in July of 1947 three months after Jackie." Sugarfoot's response sounded so informative that Leroy quickly changed directions. "Betcha you can't tell me who was the Phillies first black player?" Everyone including Dan laughed heartedly because everyone knew that the Phillies had not drafted any men of color yet, and showed no interest in doing so. "When you finish your chores Sugarfoot how 'bout a little *9 ball* for a dollar a game", Dan asked. Sugarfoot was an above average player; Dan could get some good work out of him. "Sure Dan in a minute". The four of them continue to shoot the breeze about the Negro League and its ultimate demise. Scotty, the eldest of the four, wondered if all this talk about integration was a good thing for the Negro in other facets of life. "I don't know about y'all, but integration could mean disintegration for us. Right now black folk got their businesses, their own colleges, and because they don't want us in their stores and restaurants, we spend our money with people who look like us. It's like putting a drop of chocolate syrup in a gallon of milk. I ain't gotta tell y'all who that drop of syrup is." They all nodded with approval. "Now that's what happens when you're hanging on Columbia Avenue with those Marcus Garvey People", Leroy interjected, "Bring your old ass in here and let me beat you up on this pool table."

Dan's stroke was smooth as ever. He and Sugarfoot split 4 games each, and then the phone began to ring with the daily number business. While all alone on the table, Dan decided to practice his break. As he gathered the nine balls with his back to the door, he never saw Ted Lattimore enter. "Mr. English Dan, you here might early this morning". Dan turned around and shook his hand and gave him a hug. "Hey Lattimore how you been?" "Saw your car outside, figure I'd come in to say hi." Ted responded. "Everything's cool" Dan answered, "I heard about your upcoming match with that South Philly fella." Dan was impressed with his ability to gather news so quickly." "Yeah I came in before the regular crowd to pick up a few quality games, you got time for a few?" Dan asked. "No I'm just passing through, you don't need no practice man, I seen this cat play before, he's good but you shouldn't have no problem. In fact, I'm so sure of that, if you want I can shave some of the five grand wager off for you." Dan paused at the request and took a moment to think about it. Shaving means he'll stake a portion of the bet. "I appreciate your confidence Ted and normally for a bet this size it would be a good idea, but I'm gonna go it alone on this one my friend." Ted shook his hand "Good luck Dan, but you got skill you don't need luck", as he smiled and left the pool hall. Dan stood by the door, and watched him pull away from the curb. He thought about the vote of confidence that was just bestowed upon him and it made him feel a little better about this match. However, that feeling left as quickly as it came because he knew P.J. Anderson was not going to go away easily.

The heroin deal the Andersons agreed on with Louie Appellini, put a tremendous strain on their internal family. After that terrible beating P.J. put on his childhood friend, everyone began to distance themselves from P.J. His father, Peter Anderson Sr., saw the writing on the wall. He knew it was just a matter of time before his beloved son would decide to part ways with the family. Peter explored all of the avenues necessary to convince his son to stick to the original plan, but P.J. was enjoying the life of a major drug dealer too much. The two shipments they agreed upon went as planned. The Andersons would make almost one million dollars from the deal. The only part of the agreement that remained was to introduce Louie and his organization, to a person qualified to continue what Peter and his brothers started. Peter never really bothered to search for a replacement, because he knew that one day in the very near future, P.J. would ask for his blessings, and permission to be that replacement and join up with Louie Apples.

Ever since that horrific encounter with one of his best lieutenants, P.J. found himself working harder. He still had Harry T, but Willie proved to be more of a liability since then. P.J. had to hit the streets himself to collect and distribute. Things got so busy, he didn't have any time to think about the upcoming pool match. However, Willie made sure he didn't forget. He talked about the match, and his dislike for English Dan every day.

The beginning of the week went awfully slow, and then all of a sudden it was Friday. Dan got up as usual, and had breakfast, but he went back to his apartment immediately afterwards. He wanted to give his mother and father ample enough time to depart for work, so that he could open his stash without being disturbed. His brother, John signed up for another 4 years in the Navy and was in San Diego. Even though the match wasn't until 8 o'clock, Dan wanted to count and separate the five thousand dollars. As soon as he begins to count, Amy's voice of reason and responsibility kept popping into his head. He couldn't shake the thought of her so he decided to give her a call, but then he remembered that she just started a new job as a seamstress, and would not be home until after six o'clock in the evening. Dan counted ninety-two hundred dollars. "Wow" he thought. He spent a lot time and energy to accumulate this bread and more than half could be lost within an hour's time. That thought alone brought chills up his spine. He separated the five, and put it in a brown paper bag, and counted another two hundred for his pocket. "Hey", he said to himself, "I might lose, don't wanna be in the streets with no dough." He put the remaining back in his stash, and tried to put all those negative thoughts out of his mind, and envisioned his stash bulging with five more thousand dollars.

The 1952 Oldsmobile hugged the curves of East River Drive, and it seemed like Dan literally floated down town. He parked a couple of blocks away from Broad and South Streets. No one knew what kind of car he drove, and he wanted to keep it like that. The corner was alive with its usual Friday night revelry, as Dan made his way to Rodman Street, and turned the corner. The pool hall was mobbed, and he slipped in virtually unnoticed. "I told you that sucker wasn't coming let's get the hell outta here P.J.", shouted Willie. Dan made his way over to Chick Davis, and handed him the brown paper bag. "Hold your tongue Willie we got ourselves a match tonite," Chick said with delight. The crowd was ecstatic. Dan scanned the crowd and spotted Amy and Charlotte standing near the center table. He nodded their way with a slight smile. They both waved. Chick motioned to his detective friend, and walked behind the counter to count the wagers. P.J. had already given Chick his bag and he counted out 10,000 dollars. He took his bet fee of $300.00 and put the remaining $9700.00 in one of the bags and gave it to Detective Washington.

He took the cover off the center table, and quickly got the crowd's attention. "These two fine gentlemen are ready give you all what you've been waiting for. The best five out of seven games of nine ball". At that moment, P.J. walked over to Chick and whispered in his ear. "Hold on we have a slight change here." Chick continued, "If it's alright with English Dan, P.J. would rather play straight pool to 100 points." That brought a big smile to Dan's face, "Don't much matter to me what we play, we can play a game of jacks for this money, and I'm still gonna whip his ass!" The crowd roared with laughter including P.J. The only one that wasn't laughing was Amy. She sat there hoping this night turns out in Eddie Gordon's favor.

They volleyed with the cue ball for the chance to shoot first and Dan won. He paused for a few seconds and looked at the fine workmanship of the table. That seemed to settle his nerves and he broke and three balls fell. Chick's other helper, Elliott, stood by the counter and slid three over to the right. Dan loved to hear that clacking sound the counter made, as he continued shoot and ran the whole rack and 6 more on the next rack. "twenty to zero" Elliot announced. P.J. chalked up his cue stick and went to work. His stroke was smooth as silk. Dan found himself enjoying his skills, considering it was the first time he saw him shoot. The more balls he knocked down, the harder he shot. It seemed to bring him delight to hear the cracking sound of the balls crashing into the pocket. Elliot could barely keep up with P.J.'s pace. The crowd was star struck. They oohed and aahed with every motion P.J. made. He was still their hero, and he would not disappoint. P.J. ran 40 balls before he missed. Dan took a sigh of relief and he wondered if he would ever miss. "20 to 40" Elliot bellowed. Dan realized he had to slow the pace of the game down and keep Mr. Anderson on the sideline. As P.J. laughed and joked with his buddies, Dan deliberately took his time and ran three racks. It wasn't exciting and the crowd got restless, and even more important, it frustrated the hell out of P.J. "62 to 40" announced Elliot. P.J.'s neatly processed hair began to unravel, as he took aim and began to pocket balls at his rapid pace. However, the slowdown threw his concentration off and he missed after dropping ten balls. The score was now 62 to 50. Dan saw a golden opportunity to widen the gap and take control of this game. He continued to shoot at that same deliberate pace, but now his "pool shooter's ego" had him playing for the crowd. Dan made dazzling bank shots and passed up easy shots for more difficult ones. The crowd responded and showed their appreciation with delightful clamor. He even winked at Amy and Charlotte in between shots. When Dan finally missed, the score was 92 to 50. Now mostly everyone in the hall figured the game was over in just a matter of time. But Dan's antics in front of his South Philly crowd, furiated P.J. and woke him up. P.J. stopped smiling and clowning around, and began to shoot. He knocked off the first rack that changed the score to 92 to 64. After P.J. pocketed another one, the fickle crowd began to sway back in his direction. P.J. continued to make shots and now Dan grew antsy when Elliot shouted "92 to 86". Dan also realized why P.J. chose *straight pool* over *9-ball* because of his ability to stay focused in a long grueling match. Most cats would have faded by now, but P.J. had found his second wind and headed for the home stretch.

The crowd silently watched Blue rack the 14 balls, and anyone who could perform elementary math knew that P.J. could reach 100 points on this rack, and English Dan may not get another shot. P.J. knocked down the first four balls easily then began to tackle the more difficult shots. "Five ball corner left" P.J. shouted. "One ball corner right!" One more hard shot and the table would be wide open. The score was tied 92 to 92, and P.J. was more focused than ever. He settled his nerves and slowly took aim. The crowd was deafly silent. Dan could do nothing but watch. He looked over at Amy and she hung her head down in despair. P.J. drew his cue back and just as he connected with the cue ball, Willie blurted out "Finish him off!" He had listened to Willie all week, bad mouthing Dan, until the very sound of his voice had become irritating. This sudden outburst caused him to hit the ball slightly off, and P.J. missed the shot. While still in the shooting position, P.J. glared in the direction of Willie, and shook his head in utter disgust. The crowd was ghastly disappointed, and turned their ire towards Willie. Chick Davis had to settle the pool hall down so that the game could continue. Willie slipped out the door, while he was still in good health. Elliot announced the score "92 to 92"!

Dan took a sigh of relief, but his work was not over. P.J.'s miss left nine balls on the table. Dan needed to pocket eight of them. He took a deep breath, and methodically went to work. No fancy shots, no playing to the crowd. Dan knew he could not give P.J. another chance. He made the cue ball do exactly what he wanted. Left-side English, right-side English, the ball made a screeching halt when Dan saw the need. By the time he pocketed the eighth and final ball, the crowd was so appreciative of his precise skills they almost forgot their native son, P.J., was on the losing end of this fantastic match. Dan immediately walked over to P.J. and shook his hand. P.J. was gracious in defeat and said "English Dan, you shoot a hellava game." The crowd applauded hearing their hero's gracious comment. Dan humbly nodded, and walked over to Chick and Detective Williams handed Dan the brown bag, and Chick gave Dan a hearty handshake and whispered in his ear, "My friend Mr. Washington can walk you to your car, if you wish." Dan thanked him and replied, "I'll be fine." While everyone was excited by what they just witnessed, Dan put the bag in his jacket pocket and zippered it. He then reached into his pants pocket and gave Blue and Elliot twenty dollars each. He walked over to Amy, and discreetly gave her the remaining $160.00 and told her he'll call her later. Charlotte wanted to chat, but Dan elected to slip out of Chick's Pool Room, almost as quietly as he came in.

As Dan reached the top step, the late spring night air felt refreshingly good. He thought about the amazing task he had just accomplished, but Dan was not naïve. The task was not over until the brown bag was safely put back in his stash. His car was parked at 13th and Lombard Streets, two blocks away. He decided to slip down Rodman Street to 13th, and proceed left to Lombard Street. Even though it was well past ten o'clock in the evening, he wanted to bypass the Broad and South Streets crowd. Dan began to walk down the street at a steady pace. Halfway down the block he wondered why he refused Chick's offer for an escort. At that split second, Dan saw two men turn the corner and proceeded toward him. They did not run, but they were walking very fast. Dan instinctively crossed to the left side of the street, hoping this would at least force the two to show their intent. Instead the two shadowy figures slowed down as if they were unsure what to do next. Suddenly a voice from an unseen person behind them shouted "what the fuck y'all waiting for, get'em." Dan tightened up in preparation for what was to come. He thought about turning and running the opposite direction, when the screeching sound of a car, and its bright headlights changed his mind. A dreaded feeling of despair overcame him. It wasn't the fear of the physical confrontation, but the fear of losing his bread he worked so hard and long for, to a couple of assholes. The car continued to come down the street, and the two would be highway men continue towards him. Dan didn't want to take his eyes off of the men. However, the bright headlights made them hesitate, and gave Dan just enough time to allow his peripheral vision to glance at the car. While trying to get a clear picture of the driver and his intent, the men start running at a rapid pace towards Dan with guns drawn. The window of the car slowly went down, and Lattimore said in a matter of fact kind of way, "Figured you might need a ride tonight." Dan made his way to the passenger side while keeping his eyes on the two men. As he opened the door, Ted removed a black .45 semi-automatic handgun from his seat, and Dan took a big sigh of relief. He tried to get a look at the identities of the two men but Lattimore sped past them too fast and turned down 13th street. "Where is your car Dan?" "Right around the corner Ted", Dan replied feeling very grateful.

"Let me go around the block a few times, and give your two buddies a chance to clear the neighborhood. I do wanna have to kill one of those motherfuckers tonight." Dan just nodded his head in approval. "Since you wouldn't let me stake some of that cash, the least I could do is to make sure the purse got back to North Philly safely". "I am truly grateful my friend; how can I repay you?" "Don't worry about it. I peeped in on you to see how you were doing, and just like I predicted, you were handling your business so I decided to wait outside to make sure everything else went as smooth". Dan did not respond. His nerves were settled now and he began to ponder who that unseen person was, and who else was behind this? Ted continued, "I tell you what you can do, how bout you come on the road with me for a week or so. There's a string of pool halls from Boston through New York, and even down to Baltimore that a couple good shooters like you and I can still make a few bucks." The very sound of that excited Dan, he had heard of cats going on the road, but never had the opportunity to experience it. "That sounds great! When would you like to go?" Dan responded enthusiastically. "Meet me at the car lot at around ten o'clock Monday morning, we'll both put about $2500.00 each, and hustle from the five grand and at the end we'll split the profits. Oh yeah, pack enough rags for about a week."

Dan settled in his shiny Oldsmobile, and turned on the radio. The sweet sound of Ella Fitzgerald engulfed the car's interior. Dan was in no hurry to get home, so he decided to take the West River Drive. He had just accomplished a herculean task tonight; he beat one of the best pool shooters he has ever faced for a hefty five thousand dollars. He let that thought swirl around in his head for a few minutes as the Olds swerved around the river bank curves. When he turned the corner of Diamond Street and his apartment was in sight, he whispered to himself, "Dan don't you ever turn down a police escort again."

Dan woke up to the smell of Philadelphia scrapple frying on the stove. It was Saturday morning and his parents did not have to work. His mother refused to take "no" for an answer so Dan was compelled to have breakfast with them. He had not talked to his Mom and Dad in a few days so it turned out to be a good idea. "Mom, I'm going on the road with a friend for a few days to play pool". "You be careful boy", she replied with that southern drawl. "Call us to make sure you are okay", his Father insisted. Will do, Dan responded as the three of them took a moment out of their busy schedules, and enjoyed the company of each other over a home cooked breakfast.

CHAPTER 7

Hitting The Road

———

THE VERY THOUGHT OF GETTING out of the city for a few ticks was exciting in itself, not to mention the chance to make a few bucks playing the game English Dan truly loved. When he arrived at the Lattimore Oldsmobile car dealership, Ted was giving one of his top salesman instructions to be carried out in his absence. He noticed Dan, and pointed to a parking space separate from his inventory. Dan admired Ted as he glanced at his ever present Cordovan Penny Loafers. He didn't know much about him but what he did know warranted much respect. As Dan loaded his bags into the trunk, the sight of the holstered 45 automatic confirmed one thing, he wouldn't wanna be the person that ever disrespected him.

"We're gonna head up to Boston first and work our way down" as he turned on to Route One.

"Have you thought about who tried to cross you Friday night?" "Thought about it a lot", Dan replied. "The first person one would consider was my opponent, P.J., the stick-up would be like an insurance policy, if he lost the game, he'll just take it back. But that's not in his character, heard some bad stories about him, but a back alley strong arm man, he's not. However, a few people in his organization sure fit the description like his asshole sidekick, Willie. I would even lay odds it was him."

Ted was paying attention to the morning traffic, but intently listening to Dan's assessment of Friday night's events. "You have a pretty good judge of character for a young fella. Had some of my people look into that night's fiasco, and you are right, it was Willie who orchestrated the whole thing. P.J. had nothing to do with it, and if he had known Willie would be in a heap of trouble. Nonsense like that makes it hard for a couple of pool hustlers like you and I". Dan did not respond, he was wondering how Mr. Lattimore stays so informed to the happenings on the streets and from the tone of his voice, Willie probably needs to tread very carefully. Dan's head was still swirling with excitement about Friday night's pool match and the anticipation of this road trip. Questions about the attempted robbery, and the mysteriously well informed Mr. Lattimore was a bit much for the young 22-year-old. After about 15 minutes on the highway, Dan slipped off into a well needed rest.

Theodore Robert Lattimore was born in Philadelphia in 1912, in a well-kept beautiful three story brick house at 5th and Pine Streets. The Lattimore family name with its Northern roots can be traced back to the 1700's. Fortunately, they never had to endure the hardships of slavery. In fact, they were brought to the Colonies by an English Shipbuilder and worked in his shipyard. When the Revolutionary War ended and England was forced out, the United States was established. Ironically, the Declaration of Independence did not apply to the thousands of Northern bound Blacks, who had to scramble and obtain *Freedom Papers*, to avoid being sold to opportunistic Southern landowners. The Lattimores were granted these necessary papers and expanded their expertise as shipbuilders and became the region's sailmakers. Their business blossomed and the family business grew tremendously as did their wealth.

When another Philadelphia Black-owned wealthy sailmaker, the Fortens, began to divert its energy into the abolition of slavery, the Lattimores' foresight sent them in another direction. The steam engine first came on the scene in 1825. The Lattimores knew it was just a matter of time before all ship travel would turn to steam. They opened a steam pipe manufacturing plant that supplied shipbuilders, as well as the commercial construction industry. After the Civil War and the Advent of the Industrial Revolution, once again, the Lattimores were the benefactors of the country's progress. The huge factories and plants were all powered by steam.

Young Theodore and Anne, his young sister of two years, grew up in the *upper social circle* of Black Philadelphia. However, Theodore loved to hang out with *regular folk* as much as he could. When it was time for him to be enrolled in school, he begged his father and mother to send him to public school. They bluntly ignored his request, and sent him to the private prestigious, Friends School System. Ironically the Quakers, with all of their anti-slavery positions, just began allowing coloreds into their school system.

There was only one other Black in the entire school, but Ted as he now preferred to be called, had no problems fitting in. In fact, once he realized his privileged lifestyle was not a curse, he began to enjoy and eventually excel academically and socially.

The racially polarized school was not without incidents, but once again, Ted did well. He even came to the aid of a white classmate, when a few of the school's bullies jumped Allen Dozier. They both fought off the attackers and the two fifth graders became close friends.

One day after school, Allen invited Ted over to his house, and that was the very first time Ted saw a pool table. At eleven years old, the table seemed enormous. The fine crafted polished wood gleamed and Ted fell in love. Allen's father, Cardwell, a first generation immigrant from England, immediately liked Theodore and every time he visited, he taught him the *fine science* of billiards as Mr. Cardwell called it. Back in England, Mr. Cardwell's father was a billiard master, and it was mandatory for everyone in the Dozier mansion, even the females to learn billiards. Allen, Ted's classmate never cared too much for the game, but the attention Ted was receiving from his father, forced young Allen to learn, and eventually like the game. The more they played the better they got. Allen's pool shooting ability plateaued as a teenager, however Theodore's skill and passion for the game excelled.

The two classmates remained very close all through high school. Their families even became friends and when Allen chose Harvard as his college choice, Theodore's family urged him to go also. They surely could afford it, and Ted's grades were more than qualifying, but Ted had grown tired of being the *only black*, and instead went to Lincoln University. He graduated with a Business Administration degree and enmeshed himself into the family business.

Not long after graduation, Ted married into another wealthy Black Philadelphian family. The Dows were prominent caterers and their beautiful daughter, Isabel fell in love. Young Ted was lukewarm to the idea of being married and raising a family, and his aging father and struggling business forced him to focus on these matters.

The rest of the country was waist-deep in the Depression, however Franklin Roosevelt's Economic Plans were beginning to take effect, and the tide was gradually receding. Construction projects were picking up, as were the need for steam pipes. The Lattimore Family Business was on the climb again, but the Unions were becoming more and more powerful, and their segregated policies began to slam the door on Negro workers and Negro-owned companies. Theodore's foresight, after convincing his ill father, allowed them to sell the business at a huge profit, and he took his proceeds and opened up a car dealership. Ted told his father, "People are going to drive cars for a very long time".

Ted's marriage seemed to have gotten lost on his list of priorities. They bore no children and after an amicable divorce, Isabel stated, "I bear no hard feelings, besides I could never replace his first love, shooting pool, anyway."

Allen Dozier would eventually graduate from Harvard's Law School with several corporate law firms courting his presence. He chose to stay in the Boston area, and married his college sweetheart, Megan. His tremendous success allowed him to become a major partner in the construction of a beautiful country club and golf course in the suburb of Cambridge. The first thing he did was to install three custom designed pool tables in the clubhouse.

The country club was for his wife and her friends, but the pool tables were for his beloved father, and his childhood friend, Ted Lattimore.

Dan began to toss, and turn in the midst of arousing from his deep slumber. However, before he could open and focus his eyes, the rich aroma of lilac flowers captivated his sense of smell. It was springtime in New England, one of the most beautiful places in the country, if not the world. Dan was in amazement by the rich lust of the countryside. He was born down South, but for the most part Dan was a city boy, as he twisted and turned in the seat at the sights, sounds and smells of the New England terrain.

Ted just smiled, "It had that effect on me the first time I saw it. I come up here as much as I can." Dan was also glad he came, just to be out of the city, gave him a refreshing sense of clarity. "We're gonna make a stop, get some gas, a bite to eat, and then head into Boston. I know a pretty good hotel on the dark-side of town where we can change our clothes." "Dark Side?" Dan interjected. "Yeah, son this ain't Mississippi, but it's still 1952", Ted quipped. The hotel was more than adequate and the service was top shelf. As soon as Dan got in the room he called his Mom and Pop, and then he called Amy.

The sun was beginning to set in the western skyline, as Ted pulled the Oldsmobile onto the highway. After about ten minutes of driving, Dan noticed they were out of the city, and in the suburbs. As Ted passed through a gate titled *Alden Country Club*. Dan's curiosity had peaked, "I thought we were going to a pool room", Dan questioned. "We are my friend, we are", Ted replied. The manicured grass was freshly cut, and the aroma was intoxicating. Off to the left was a golf course and to the right was a beautifully designed clubhouse with about a half dozen fancy cars parked outside. "You sure about this Ted?" Dan asked. "You better be sure, Dan cause some of these cats can shoot a good game of *9-ball*."

As Ted opened the trunk to retrieve their betting cash, he counted out one thousand dollars and gave it to Dan. "Ted", Dan intervened, "I have a long standing policy never to carry more than five hundred dollars into a pool hall. I figure, if I can't beat you with five, I can't beat you." Ted pondered the statement, and Dan continued. "I tell you what, we'll take five a piece, and if at any time we run into a hotshot, we'll decide to return to the trunk and get more." Ted nodded his head in approval; however, he wasn't accustomed to taking advice, even though it was good advice.

It was well after regular hours, and all of the country club's staff had gone home. The club house was immaculate, and on the weekends it was always crowded with members, and their families and friends. However, during the week, it was a perfect escape from the humdrums of family life, and a getaway after a hard day at the office. After Allen Dozier installed the pool tables, he was quite surprised by the quality of shooters, the three custom design tables attracted.

"Theodore Robert Lattimore! It's been too long, how long has it been?" questioned Allen. They embraced and then shook hands. "Is this the young phenom, you been bragging about?" "Allen how have you been replied", Ted? "Yes, this is my man, English Dan." Dan shook his hand, and looked around the large spacious room. The first thing he noticed was the three beautiful pool tables. The next thing he noticed were the seven or so white gentlemen that did not seemed to share the same hospitable enthusiasm as Allen. "You still are drinking Scotch, Ted? How about you Dan, what can I get you?" "'Er, just a coke, a coke will be just fine, as Dan tried to at least appear comfortable." "Make yourselves at home, bellowed Allen. Don't pay these guys any attention", referring to the white men." "Fellas, these two gentlemen are my guest tonight, and I expect you to treat them as such. They don't wanna marry your daughters, and they surely have no desire to steal your ugly wives", Allen with a slight laugh. A couple of the gentlemen loosened up, and laughed however one cat turned as red as a beet, and grabbed his jacket and quietly left. "Don't worry about Charles, he can't shoot anyway, but if the rest of you distinguished gentlemen choose to stay, you just might learn a little about the fine science of pool, and who knows, you might even make a few bucks." Ted walked over to the men and introduced himself. There were two judges and a police chief and the rest were lawyers. Dan walked over to the cue stick rack and grabbed a stick. He couldn't wait to try out the tables. As Ted and Allen got reacquainted over a couple of drinks at the bar, Dan walked over to one of the tables and introduced himself to a middle aged balding cat. "I'm Dan, this is a mighty fine table" caressing the polished wood. "Would you like to play a little *9-ball* for let's say fifty bucks a game?" "Son, you don't waste no time, I'm Dave Johnson. Over at the Watertown Police Department, they call me Police Chief Johnson." His introduction had a cynical tone as if all black people are intimidated by the police. "I'll tell you what young fella, how 'bout we play for one hundred dollars a game?" Dan didn't blink, he grabbed two cue balls and handed one to Police Chief Johnson. Chief Johnson won the volley and broke. The number three and five balls fell into the pockets. As he chalked up his cue stick, he looked at Dan and laughed. "You fellas drove a long way for a pool game, ain't no pool halls where you come from?" It wasn't a question that demanded an answer, it was just a touch of sarcasm. Dan just smiled trying to size up his portly opponent, as Dave pocketed the one and the two balls. He shuffled to the other side of the table, and quietly ran the other four balls, leaving the nine ball in perfect position. "You boys came up here thinking this was gonna be easy", he said with that famous New England accent, and knocked down the last ball. As Dan reached in his pocket and counted out five twenties, he said to himself, "Out of all the cats in the room, I had to pick on the sharp shooter." "You wanna play another one, Mr. English Dan?"

Ted and Allen were still at the bar, while the other gentlemen suddenly took interest in Dave and Dan's game. They knew of Dave's ability, but their curiosity was aimed towards the tall dapper colored guy from North Philly. Dan was still a little nervous, and missed on the only shot he got in the next game, and Chief Johnson pocketed another hundred dollars. The second payoff caught the attention of Ted, and he and Allen walked over to the table. "You gentlemen taking advantage of this youngster", Ted said with a laugh. "No sir wouldn't do that just showing him a little New England fine hospitality. Maybe the presence of his partner helped calm him down, and Dan eked out a win on the 3rd game. The victory gave him a touch of confidence, and suddenly the glitzy country clubhouse was just a regular pool hall. Dan broke, and the nine ball fell. Ted applauded quietly, and the other spectators appreciated it also. While Dave counted out the five twenties, one of the lawyers shouted "bet you a hundred you can't do that again!" "Hold on fellas", Ted interrupted, "I'm so confident in my man English Dan, we'll bet you cats 5 hundred", as Ted put four hundred, waiting for Dan to put the other one. On a normal day in a pool hall, Dan wouldn't think about covering a bet like that, even if it was just five bucks, but this wasn't a normal day, and it sure wasn't a normal pool hall. Dan backed his partner's play and tossed his one hundred on top of Ted's four. Three of the other gentlemen counted out one hundred each and tossed it on the pile. Now everyone's attention was on Police Chief Johnson. "Stranger" referring to Ted, "You are mighty confident in this youngster. I am also mighty curious, so I guess I'll have to put up to see if this fella can do this again."

Dave racked the nine balls a little more methodical this time making sure the rack was good and tight. Dan chalked up his cue stick as his audience stood deafly silent. He sized up the cue ball and with a smooth steady stroke the cue ball crashed into the pile of nine and the three ball fell in the right corner pocket and the rest of the balls scattered. The nine ball bounced off of the six ball and slowly dropped in the left side pocket. Ted smiled and picked up the one thousand dollars as Dave reached in his pocket and paid Dan his initial $100.00 bet. The gentlemen looked at each other in amazement while Allen smiled. His investment in this club was worth every dollar to have a front row seat at this.

He decided to stir up the pot a little more. "Ted, your partner is sharp but I got two hundred that says he won't do that again and this would give you guys, referring to the four gentlemen a chance to get your money back". This time they were more hesitant, but three of them put up the one hundred dollars to make the bet five again. Dave decided this time not to bet and said, "If this fella makes that shot one more time, I might have to get my gun." The statement brought laughter to everyone and even Dan mustered a slight grin. Dan positioned his cue stick looking for the right spot on the cue ball, as his captive audience looked on. The cue ball crashed into the others as it did before, but then this time the only ball that went in the left corner pocket was the nine ball. The place went crazy, as Ted calmly picked up the wager. "You boys some kind of trick shot hustlers or something", Dave growled. He was not going to let them talk him into another game. "Let me buy you a drink Mr. English Dan" as he grabbed Dan by the shoulder and they walked over to the bar. Everyone else joined them and they talked and laughed for next two hours. They were gracious losers and Allen Dozier was the perfect host. As he walked Ted and Dan to the parking lot, he said "Ted, don't let this be the last time you come see me and Dan they're gonna talk about those shots for a very long time. You must come back and teach me how to do that."

The first thing Ted said when they got in the car was "Before you teach him, you gotta teach me. How in the hell did you make those shots? I never did anything like that before in my life". Dan confessed, "It was all luck." The statement caused both of them to break out in a hearty laugh. The first leg of this *road trip* went without a hitch, and they pocketed a total of twelve hundred dollars. The action in New York wouldn't pick up until Thursday, so they decided to stay in the Boston area for two more days and take in some of the sights. They even went to the popular Fenway Baseball Park to see the Boston Red Sox.

CHAPTER 8

Taking A Bite Out of The Apple

———

THERE'S SOMETHING VERY SPECIAL ABOUT this tiny string of islands connected by bridges, and tunnels. Every section of New York, and every neighborhood can be defined by the hard-working people who reside there: Brooklyn, Bedford Stuyvesant, the Bronx, Queens, Long Island, Staten Island and busy downtown Manhattan. They all bring a very unique flavor to the mixture that is New York. However, when you cross 110th Street, you enter into what many have called, "The Soul of New York City." Harlem is the pulse and heartbeat of the city, steaming with rich, cultural, and artistic icons. To those who are less in tuned, Harlem is where "the coloreds live" but to the more mindful, Harlem is "Mecca", an ornate center piece in one of the world's famous cities. Harlem is home to the best of the best, the best doctors, technicians and the best regular folk all striving to raise their families. Harlem is also home to the best gangsters and criminals, and this broad array of people all pass through *Sonny's Pool Hall* on 125th Street between 8th & 9th Avenues where Harlem's best and may be some of the world's best pool hustlers reside.

As Ted pulled the Oldsmobile into a parking space around the corner from Sonny's, Dan was speechless like most first time visitors are at the energy and the tremendous amount of people on the streets. Dan saw many movie scenes of a busy New York City, but to be up close was mind boggling. The streams of people seemed to never end. Ted allowed Dan to take in the sights for a few minutes, and then he reiterated, "I know you been in a lot of pool halls, Dan and for the most part they're all the same, but Sonny's attracts some of the sharpest hustlers on the East Coast. Figured I'd just let you know and one more thing, (as he opened the trunk), I know you don't go for the fancy pool cues, but this place is so busy, the house cues are all worn out." As Ted reached into the trunk and gave Dan a sparking new wood grain cue stick case. He then took out his own cue case, and without forethought or comment took a small snob nosed .38 revolver that lay near the big .45 automatic and placed the revolver inside a tiny compartment in his cue stick case. He then said sarcastically, "I know, only 500 dollars apiece", as they pocketed the cash and walked around the corner towards the heralded Sonny's Pool Hall. Dan didn't reply, he was still mesmerized by the atmosphere but he sure would like to know how many more guns does his penny loafer wearing friend keep in his trunk.

The stores and shops along 125th Street were stacked three stories and sometimes four stores high and they were all eager to attract the thousands of people who pass by them every day. As Ted and Dan began to climb the stairs, Dan who had been mostly quiet said, "listen up Ted in order to maximize our ability over the next two days, we must stay away from the high rollers the very first day and concentrate on the lessor competition, if they size us up, as too hard to beat, the heavy bettors won't come near us." Ted nodded with approval, though this approach never applied to him. He went to pool halls with the burning desire to play the best player in the house. He was motivated by the challenge, however Dan had to be more practical and his motivation was more simple, cash.

It was only three o'clock, and the place was already packed. As Ted nodded and shook hands with a few acquaintances, Dan was surveying the talent and the tables. The game of choice seemed to be *nine ball,* and the trash talk was plentiful. Dan thought if these cats can shoot as well as they talk, it's going to be a long night. The names were as colorful as some of the outfits. A cat name Mississippi was taking advantage of the young boy named Scooter. On another table the Uptown Kid was being ravaged by Billy Boy and Black Sam, all dressed up in dazzling red outfit, had everyone's attention with his big mouth and his game. "Nigga you must've bumped your head. What you had a dream that you beat Black Sam on the pool table last night, well let me tell you, a dream is all it was." He counted what appeared to be twenty dollars as he paused to wait for his opponent to rack the next game.

Displaying a gold filled grin Sam, shouted over to the other table "Hey Mississippi, we got us a couple of visitors." It was not hard to distinguish Ted and Dan from the rest of the crowd. Dan was his usual dapper self and Ted was conservatively dressed with a shiny pair of black penny loafers. "Yeah", Sam continued, "they got some fancy cue stick cases too. You fellas aim on partaking in the fine science of billiards?" The crowd let out a short burst of laughter. Everyone there were pool hustlers and the term billiards was a bit sophisticated for this crowd. But the touch of sarcasm even amused Ted. "How about it", Sam continued, "cause this cat here is just about broke", referring to his present opponent. At first the attention was on the both of them but after sizing up the two, Sam now was leaning more towards the older, Mr. Ted Lattimore. Sam was loud but not stupid. The young lean, confident English Dan appeared to be the tougher of the two. As Sam made quick work of his opponent and he gave Sam what appeared to be his last twenty dollars, Ted quietly opened his case and assembled his cue stick. He then placed the case on top of the soda machine. "How much is this game gonna cost me Sam?" Ted asked. "A double saw buck my friend", he answered with a wide smile.

Dan was itching to play himself, but he had not seen Ted play since that night he beat him out his cash and his car, so he decided to be a spectator for a few ticks. Nothing fell when Black Sam broke the rack of nine balls and Ted went to work. Sam's loud banter continued as Ted silently pocketed balls one through five rather easily. The six ball was in bad spot, so Ted decided to place defense, and put the cue ball in a place that gave his boisterous opponent no shot. This infuriated Sam immediately. "Did you see that shit Mississippi, Mr. Penny Loafers is trying to hide the cue ball"? Sam then tried a very difficult shot on the 6 ball and missed, but in doing so opened up the table and Ted pocketed balls six through nine and won the game. Sam grumbled as he handed Ted the wager. "I don't appreciate what you just did as he began to rack the balls for the next game." Dan saw loud mouth losers before, but this cat made Dan look in the direction of Ted's case above the soda machine.

Ted was not fazed at all. He chalked up his cue stick and methodically won the next four games and Black Sam called it quits and walked away whimpering. One would think at first sight, that Sam was some big time street hustler, but he was just a regular working stiff, and if he had lost anymore of his paycheck, you would have heard his wife's mouth up and down Lennox Avenue.

After watching Ted for two games, Dan was drawn over to Mississippi's table. Mississippi's story was a bit more intriguing than Black Sam's, and it demands to be told. It seem like it was yesterday when he arrived in New York City, but that was ten years ago.

After the slaves were freed, the Great Northern Migration began. They sought refuge in the big cities, and little towns north of the Mason Dixon. Upon their arrival, some embraced their new home, and the challenges that came with it. However, some immediately disliked it, and returned to the world they were more comfortable with. Also within that migration, were those who were forced to leave, with lynch mobs, or law enforcement, nipping at their heels, this group had no choice, but to accept their new environment. Many of them learned to love their northern safe havens, but many from that group would spend a lifetime brooding over their involuntary displacement.

Mississippi was a member of the first group. He had no regrets. He loved the life he made for himself, and he loved New York. Born John Glover, in Montgomery Alabama, on a cotton farm, one would think Mississippi's choice was an easy decision. Who would want to endure the hard work and drudgery of a life on a cotton farm, working from sunrise to sunset, in the scorching Alabama heat? Sure an easy decision, but that was not the situation. First of all, Mississippi was not born on a cotton farm, it was a cotton plantation, a plantation that was owned by his grandfather, a white rich land Baron, which was the source of his fair skin, and his father's wealth.

Mississippi's grandfather, Matthew Glover, was up in age when he did something unheard of in his time. He fell in love with a young Negro sharecropper named Mary Beth, and married her. Going against the wishes of his family, friends, and business associates, Matthew meticulously had his attorney draft the proper documents that made Mary Beth, the sole heir to his entire estate. "Why not", he thought. His first wife died years before of small pox and their only son was killed in one of the early Civil War battles. He dreaded the thought of leaving his fortune to some distant relatives, or even worse to an opportunistic land grabber. His mind was made up.

Mary Beth bore him one son, Mississippi's father, Matthew Jr. His grandfather taught his young wife everything there was to know about the cotton industry. He even told her what to expect when he died. By the time of his death, Matthew Jr. was 20 years old. He stood by his mother, and together they fought off the land grabbing county assessors, the white vigilantes, and even the cotton crop *nemesis*, the boll weevil.

When Mississippi was born in 1921, the family business was flourishing. His father downsized the immense plantation, and sold off large chunks of unused land. He divided the remaining acreage, and made fair agreements with the sharecroppers. Alabama was no longer *King Cotton*, as it was in the 1800's, but the Glovers' made a decent living.

Mississippi's father made sure his young son knew the meaning of hard work, and for the most part, Johnny, as everyone called him, did well around the farm. His father taught him the agricultural side, and the administrative side of running a successful farm. By the age of 19, Mississippi, like many young men, begin to frown at the fact of being on the farm for the rest of their life. Nonetheless, Johnny never voiced his displeasure to his father. He loved and respected his father and mother. The only thing he loved more than that, was chasing girls.

Mississippi had grown up into a very handsome young man, and at 21 years old, the ladies could not keep their hands off of him. However, the ladies were not exclusively young, in fact, Johnny had the attention of many older females. His gravitation towards this selection had become increasing dangerous, because some of them were married.

Mabel Stone was very beautiful, and Mississippi was crazy about her, and she was very much in love with him. The 15-year age difference was no problem, but her insanely jealous husband was. After completing his business on the farm, Mississippi agreed to meet Mabel at a local bar. He knew it was not a good idea, but lust sometimes gets in the way of common sense. "I'm gonna catch a cab, I'll be there by seven", Mabel whispered on the phone. Her husband was 20 miles away on business, but she was so terrified of him, she would have whispered even if he were in another country.

Harold Stone was salesman and stayed on the road for weeks at a time. He knew Mabel had a *wandering eye* when he married her, but his stubborn nature told him otherwise. They were only married for three years, and he had suspected her of at least two extra marital affairs. When she laid her eyes on the handsome Johnny Glover, she had to have him. At first, they were very careful, but after a while, they did not care who saw them. Word of this got back to his father, and he adamantly warned his son of this dangerous choice. Mississippi knew his father was correct, but he was blinded by the passion the two of them shared.

He never saw Harold come through the door. When another female patron screamed, everyone turned in that direction. All Mississippi saw was a charging, angry husband, frothing at the mouth, and screaming. He also saw a shiny, straight razor in Harold's hand. His first instinct was to push Mabel out of the way. The armed Harold Stone was only a few yards away, when Mississippi grabbed a beer bottle with his right hand, and grabbed Harold's razor wielding hand with his left. As they tumbled to the floor, the bottle broke, and Mississippi pierced Harold's neck with the bottle's jagged edge, striking his jugular vein. By the time Mississippi and Mabel gathered themselves, and left the scene, Harold Stone was dead. The bottle ripped open a huge gash, and he bled out in minutes.

Mississippi calmed himself down. He put Mabel in a taxi cab. As he watched the cab disappear over the horizon, he felt sorry for her, and even for a split second, he felt sorry for Harold. Apparently, Harold was not out of town, and he simply waited until she left, and followed her.

As he pleaded to his father that it was self-defense, his mother wept silently. Matthew Glover gave his son a disgusted look, but there was no time for a tongue lashing. Mississippi stood there silently, as the wheels in his father's head began to turn. He still had a few friends in politics, and law enforcement, but the firm stances he and his mother took over the last 20 years, created more enemies, than friends. It would bring them much pleasure to put his beloved son behind bars. "You gonna have to leave Johnny", he solemnly stated. Mississippi immediately objected. He kept repeating that it was self-defense, but his father knew better. It was 1942 in Alabama, and justice surely was not a guarantee.

While his mother packed a small suitcase, his father spelled out specific instructions. "Your cousins in Chicago will meet you when your train arrives. I'm giving you enough cash that should take care of your needs for a few months, while I try to figure this out." He kissed his mother, and gave his father a slight hug. Mississippi hated letting his father down, and he did not want to leave, especially under these circumstances. He often dreamed of one day leaving Alabama and the farm, but this was a nightmare. As he entered the train station, his anger began to swell up in his head. Then for some defiant reason, maybe he was angry at himself, for getting in this mess. It could have been, his anger at his father for insisting that he go, or maybe he was just being young and 21 years old. Nonetheless, for whatever apparent reason, when Mississippi walked up to the window, he did not purchase a train ticket to Chicago, he purchased one to New York City.

CHAPTER 9

Alabama to New York Via Mississippi

THE STRING OF TRAIN CARS was long and seemed endless. Mississippi, instinctively began to walk towards the rear where the *colored cars* were. When he gave his ticket to the Negro conductor, he informed Mississippi that he was in the wrong section, and the *whites only cars* were at the front of the train. It suddenly dawned on Mississippi, the man at the ticket window thought he was white, and sold him a ticket in the white section. It brought a tiny smile to his face, as he thought of all the stories he heard about his grandfather and grandmother. He closed his eyes, and reflected on the last two days, and wondered why in the hell did he buy a ticket to New York.

Just before the train pulled in New York's Grand Central Station, Mississippi asked a Negro baggage man where could he get some reasonably priced living quarters. The baggage handler was startled at first by the question, and then after a closer look, he realized the young man sitting in the white section, was a very light skin colored cat. "Uptown in Harlem, I know a real nice clean spot, the Hoffman Hotel, off of 125th Street and Lennox Avenue." He began to write down the address for Mississippi, as he reached in his pocket and gave the baggage handler a two-dollar tip.

Mississippi did not have the time or the luxury of being mesmerized by New York's tall buildings or busy streets. He had to get settled in and call his parents to let them know he arrived safely. His father was reassured to hear his voice, but was puzzled by the "New York" part of the story. Mississippi explained it as "something I wanted to do." The explanation had the tone of a young man making a decision on his own. Mississippi promised his parents, he would keep in touch.

The Hoffman Hotel was very clean and his suite was more than adequate. Mississippi was accustomed to a very upscale standard of living, even though it was a farm. He felt comfortable in his new residence. It wasn't the more famous Hotel Theresa, where all the celebrities, and dignitaries stayed, but it was efficiently stylish. The chandeliers and the polished woodwork in the lobby were gleaming, and the service was top shelf.

The time had come for young Johnny Glover to use all of the worldly skills his father and mother taught him. In the blink of an eye, he was on his own. Other than chasing girls, Mississippi was all business, and very well organized. He immediately paid for two months rent in advance. He then took the remaining cash to a local bank, and opened an account. Having talked to his parents and settled in his new environment, Mississippi could now get excited about New York City. "Wow", he thought as he exited the bank, "Never saw this many people before in my life".

The United States had recently declared war on Japan, and Germany. As he passed the recruiting office, he was surprised at the amount of Negroes, lining up to join the army. He pondered on the fact that racism, segregation, and injustice would not deter these young black men from doing their part. This scene caught him by surprise, also because joining the army was the absolute furthest thing from his mind.

When he returned to the hotel, he noticed a gentleman hanging out at the front desk. He experienced a slight tinge of jealousy, because the clerk at the desk was beautiful, and he had already *sized* her up earlier. He waved at her, and walked towards the elevator. Mississippi's easy going personae, and good looks, had a way of attracting people. This was apparently so, when the gentleman walked over in his direction. "Young lady at the desk says you just got in town." Considering the circumstances, he left in Alabama, he did not appreciate his arrival to be public news. He gave the cat a long look over and replied, "Yea today, just got in today". He made a mental note to remind himself to have a little chat with the *Lady at the desk* about his personal business. He then began to wonder who this inquisitive gentleman was, and why was it so easy for him to get this information from the pretty clerk. Before he could ask any more questions, he blurted out, "Mississippi, I'm from Mississippi, and that's what my friends call me, Mississippi." The elevator door began to slowly open and Mississippi figured *Mr. 20 questions* had enough information, but before he could turn around to board the elevator, he extended his hand and said, "My name is Alvarez, Rico Alvarez". His handshake was genuine, and Mississippi slipped into the elevator.

He was too tired to think too much about Mr. Alvarez, and the solitude of his room and the comfort of his bed, never felt better. He laid still and allowed his thoughts to revisit the last 48 hours. The top of that list went to his parents. A gloomy feeling of disappointment overwhelmed him. It wasn't so much for his father, but watching his mother weep saddened him. He then envisioned Mabel's pretty smile, and that pepped him up a little, however just like a roller coaster ride reliving the unfortunate death of Mr. Stone, wiped out that moment of happiness.

John Glover then channeled his thoughts to the reality of his situation. He must never reveal his past to anyone. He must also tell his parents that if someone ask, where did he go? Tell them Chicago. He then made a promise to himself never again, put himself in a position to be forced to hurt someone over a female, and equally important, allow someone to hurt him. He slipped off into a well needed slumber, but not before thinking of the sassy clerk downstairs, Mr. Alvarez and his new name Mississippi.

It didn't take too long for Mississippi to find out who Rico Alvarez was. Nearly half of the hotel staff was writing numbers for Rico. Mr. Alvarez, apparently was a midlevel numbers banker. Mississippi heard of the numbers racket in Alabama, but it was just beginning to take hold in the South. The further North you went in big cities like Atlanta, Richmond, and Charleston, the policy game was more popular. Upon further inquiry, Mississippi learned that Rico was banking every bet from five dollars and below, and he had over one hundred writers turning in numbers. After applying a little arithmetic, Mississippi concluded this is a "man on the rise". The next item on his list, was to find out if Louise, the front desk clerk was romantically involved with Rico. In Mississippi's mind, and because of his yen for the opposite sex, this information was near the top of his list of priorities.

"No my man", Rico replied, when Mississippi casually yet respectfully asked him about Louise. "Go ahead young buck, she's all yours", Rico insisted. "Louise is very trustworthy, and right now, that's more important than romance. You'd be surprised what a woman can do for you, when there's no sex involved." Mississippi had been in New York a little over a week, and he saw Rico passing through the hotel, but never had the opportunity to have a meaningful conversation. "I have a pretty good eye for recognizing people", Rico added. "We must sit down some time and have lunch." Mississippi answered with an enthusiastic, "Sure we can do that."

CHAPTER 10

Choices

MISSISSIPPI COULD NOT SAY HOW trustworthy Louise Perkins was, but she was sure fantastic in the sack. New York City was proving every day to be a good choice. He knew he had more important choices to make in his life, however Louise made him feel like a normal 21-year-old again.

The Woolworth lunch counter was crowded as always. Located off of Amsterdam Avenue, right in the middle of Harlem, made it convenient, and the lunchtime specials, made it an easy choice, for the hundreds who pass through their doors every day. Rico and Mississippi managed to get a small booth in the far corner. Oblivious to the throngs of people, passing by their window view, they settled in their seats, and began chomping down on their Rueben sandwiches. It had become one of

Mississippi's favorite staple since his untimely flight from Alabama, and its country cooking. As Rico wiped the sauerkraut from his mouth, he laughed and said, "The first time I saw you, I thought you were Puerto Rican. That all changed real fast when you opened your mouth, and out came that southern draw". Mississippi managed a slight smile. Mention of his past still made him a little nervous. "Like I said before", Rico continued, "I have a pretty good eye for recognizing people". Mississippi tried not to look too anxious. "I need someone who can pick up betting slips. My enterprise is expanding faster than I planned, and it would be a great chance for a young cat like you to come on board and learn the trade." Rico paused, not waiting for a verbal response, but he wanted to see his facial, and body response. Mississippi was a promising businessman before he arrived in New York, so the idea of making money wasn't new to him. He showed no expression at all, waiting for Rico to continue. "If you need more time to think about my offer, take all the time you need."

Mississippi was a very insightful man long before circumstances brought him north to New York. The beautiful Ms. Louise Perkins was a tad inquisitive on their last date. He figured Rico asked her to find out more about the southern stranger. In doing so, she tipped her hand, and hinted that Rico was looking for a runner. Mississippi then did some investigative homework himself. He was able to find out a little more about Rico's business, and how it works, and more important, how much he was taking in. He also discovered that Rico was half Puerto Rican, and half Black. This divided heritage allowed him to work the Spanish Harlem side of town, as well as the colored side of Harlem. Mississippi estimated that his take was well over $20,000 a week. After payoffs, and overhead, Rico was probably netting about $5,000 a week. In 1942, just a few years after the Great Depression, this was not bad at all.

As Rico reached into his pocket to leave a tip, Mississippi whispered, "I need to know a few factors of grave importance. Number one, how protected is your operation? I didn't come to New York to get pinched. Number two, what about transportation, and lastly how much does the job pay?" Rico thought to himself, "Louise was right, this cat is not some regular Joe off the turnip truck." He smiled and replied, "We have ample protection from the law, and the street. Yes, a driver is assigned to take you to all of the pickup points, and how about a hundred a week for starters." "How about two hundred a week, and you got a deal", Mississippi shot back.

When Mississippi arrived in New York two months ago. The last thing on his mind was getting a job. He never approached it like that even when he was running a farm in Alabama. He was never working for his father. He was working with his father. It was no difference now, in fact he made sure he stressed that point with Rico. He treated his new found employment with the same respect, and dignity, he learned working on the cotton farm. Rico quickly recognized these qualities, and in a matter of six months, Mississippi was picking up cash receipts, and his weekly salary tripled. Rico was very pleased with the young cat's progress. It allowed him to concentrate on other areas of the business.

Mississippi spoke to his parents in Alabama, regularly. He learned that Mabel told the investigative detective, it was he who attacked her husband with a bottle, and a warrant was issued for his arrest. The charge was murder. This information did not surprise Mississippi, but it made his heart a little colder, and he was never that young romantic, girl chaser again. He only saw Louise from time to time, mostly because he moved out of the hotel into a beautiful brownstone house on Sugar Hill, and he was simply too busy.

It's been three years since Mississippi got off that train at Grand Central Station. The year is 1945, and the war is over, and troops began pouring back into the cities. One of the more popular past times for soldiers, especially in Europe, was shooting billiards. The local pool halls became bulging with pool shooters and the games popularity exploded. Everyone claimed to be a pool shark, and were willing to put hard earned money on their skills. Mississippi never played the game before moving to New York. A couple of years ago, he began to learn, and like most people, he fell in love. He found it very relaxing, and in the last few months, his skill level excelled. He also discovered he liked to watch the game just as much. Whenever he got a chance, he began spending time at the many pool halls across the city. He witnessed some of the sharpest pool shooters probably in the world. While patronizing the pool halls, Mississippi found himself rubbing elbows with some of Harlem's finest citizens, as well as Harlem's toughest. Most of the latter group, he steered clear of, but he was always looking for an opportunity to present itself. Much like it did when he met Rico, five years ago, and as a result of his insight, his business "portfolio" as he called it, began to expand.

Mississippi was very frugal, and practical with money, something he learned as a child on the farm. He managed to save over twenty thousand dollars, and still lived a rather lavish lifestyle. His townhouse was beautiful, and always insisted that his clothes be the very best. His 1942 Cadillac wasn't new, but it still turned heads when he drove by.

A very close friend of Rico needed some inventory for a potentially lucrative drug deal. Rico Alvarez never spent one night in jail, and he wanted to keep it like that. He was making more than enough for himself, and his organization, however, Pedro Cruz was childhood friend, so he agreed to help him find some investors. He explained the situation to Mississippi and two others. Rico warned them of the potential risk, as well as the return. Mississippi took a day to ponder, and calculate the offer, and only because it had the blessings of Rico, he invested twenty-five thousand dollars, with the promise of fifty thousand in 90 days. 89 days later, Pedro Cruz arrived at his townhouse, with a small satchel. Inside that satchel was fifty thousand dollars.

CHAPTER 11

The Face of Change

IN TIME, ALL THINGS WILL change. That statement is no more apparent than with the young man that stepped off that train some years ago. Left behind him, were things he hope would never resurface again, and the only family he ever knew, and loved. His parents were still the most important thing in his life, but the child they so proudly named, John Glover no longer existed. Mississippi had nearly erased his entire past away. His naturally wavy hair was cut to look like the processed hair styles the blacks made popular. His custom tailored clothes bore no resemblance of the Alabama cotton farm he was reared on. One would think he was born and raised on the streets of Harlem, and even that distinctive Southern accent was gone.

Rico Alvarez was relieved that the deal went smoothly. He was wise enough to know something like that could easily go very wrong. He invited Mississippi over to his apartment in Manhattan to have dinner. They were so busy; they haven't had the chance to talk in a while. Rico was very successful, and the key to his success was simplicity. He took care of his business, and his business took care of him.

The maid opened the door, and Mississippi strolled in, and placed his hat on a hat rack in the corner. He was quietly, yet exquisitely dressed as always. Rico smiled, he was very proud of his protégé. The two of them had come a long way. Rico's family lived in another apartment on the other side of town. This apartment was for special meetings of his inner circle, private contemplation, and an occasional dinner with close associates. As the maid disappeared in the kitchen to finish preparing dinner, Rico fixed two club sodas. Neither of them were drinkers, and they both would be the first to admit, that a clear head is one of the major factors of their success.

"I'm glad that deal between you and Pedro worked out", Rico said with a slight smile. "He and I grew up together, we are family. I'm not too crazy about his choice of business, but like I said, we are family." Mississippi has known Rico for over five years. He practically knew what was coming next. "You are a very good businessman, Miss. That's because you calculate everything you do before you do it. Now the Mississippi I have grown to know and love, did a heap of homework after that deal went off without a hitch." Mississippi could not wipe the smile off his face. Rico continued, "The potential numbers on the Heroin trade are out of the ballpark, but so are the risks, and residual trail of pain and suffering it leaves." Mississippi's expression became serious, and attentive again. "You are much too talented for that, and it's a very dirty, messy business. Your hands would get very dirty." Mississippi looked at his hands, as Rico finished. His hands were professionally manicured, and always clean and he intended to keep them like that. "However, you are a grown man, and I can only suggest to you, not to let those potential returns cloud your judgment." Mississippi knew he was correct, and yes, he weighed getting involved, but his calculations told him to stay away.

"Nice pad Mr. Alvarez", as Mississippi gazed around the spacious, and well decorated apartment, wanting to change the subject. He had learned so much from Rico in the last five years. He was truly grateful for their relationship/ "That's a nice pad you have as well", Rico shot back. "You mean my spot on Sugar Hill", Mississippi answered. "No, your house on 112th Street". There was a five second space of silence, as Mississippi took a sip of his club soda. "It's clean, well-organized, and has a nice touch of class", Rico continued. "And your employees are the best I've seen in a long time". That ever present broad smile returned to Mississippi's face.

About six months ago, Mississippi began dating a beautiful, and very talented female named, Ava. After a few dates, he learned that Ava was a very high class, woman of the night, with an exclusive clientele list. She took one look at Mississippi's soft yet dazzling features, and told him there's a gold mine waiting for him in the *oldest profession known to man*. The two of them sat down with paper and pencil, and mapped out a plan. They leased a beautiful townhouse right between Harlem and Manhattan to maximize both black and white customers. Mississippi then laid down strict rules. No drugs, and if you need to be slapped around, they could not work for him. All of the females must meet these standards, and unlike most, the females would earn a very decent percentage of the income. He put George Burris, a good friend, in charge of security. His job was to also make sure Ava was not skimming the profits. The fact that Rico made it his business to know all he could about his close associates, reassured Mississippi that he was in the right company.

"Enough about business", Rico insisted. "Are you hungry" as the maid began setting the table and bringing in the food. "Miss, there's one more point I'd like to make before we eat." Rico's tone became even and deliberate. "A wise man told me a long time ago. To do el dinero que noes suyo". Mississippi had picked up a little Spanish since meeting Rico, and he knew dinero meant money. As Mississippi pondered the translation, Rico calmly stated "all of the money is not yours".

The maid placed the dinner plates in front of Rico and Mississippi, who were now sitting at the table. The chicken masala was covered with a golden brown sauce. The mushrooms were perfectly sautéed, and side of vegetable medley made the plate look like a picture in the magazines. Mississippi remembered their first meal together, and could not resist saying "what happened to the sauerkraut, I thought we were having ruebens". Rico's outburst of laughter even caused the maid to laugh, and she had no idea what they were saying due to her lack of the English language.

Mississippi was busier than ever with the numbers, and his house on 112th Street, however he found time to play more pool, and was enjoying the game like never before. That was probably because he was getting better, and he was even making a few bucks at it. The money was nothing compared to what he was earning on the street, but it was good for his pool shooter ego. Out of all of the pool halls in Harlem, Jakes was his favorite. A shooter could get a competitive match for decent money, and if he just chose to watch, the audience would be thoroughly entertained by the quality of players that came through the door.

Mississippi had upgraded his car recently, and the 1947 Cadillac Fleetwood was beautiful. He had just finished his rounds, as the autumn sunset gradually dimmed the Harlem skyline. He climbed the stairway of Jakes, not eager to play, just wanting to unwind after a long day. He waved at a few friends, and shot the breeze with the owner Jake. Jake

Epstein was aging and it was rumored he was trying to retire, hoping to lease the place to someone else. Mississippi suddenly saw something he had not seen in a long time. At the corner table, he gazed at two white cats shooting pool.

It was not unheard of for whites to venture this far up Harlem socially, but it was rare. His curiosity forced him over to the table to get a closer look. They were playing *9-ball* for twenty bucks a game. The taller gentleman seemed to be the better player, but neither of them were hustlers. They seemed to be just enjoying themselves. Mississippi immediately calculated that these cats couldn't be regular working folk, because it was still 1948, and twenty dollars was a half weeks' wage at a decent job, and full week paycheck at other places of employment. As he turned to walk away, the taller gentleman asked, "You wanna partake in a little *9-ball?* My younger brother isn't much competition". The request caught Mississippi by surprise, but what was even more surprising was his vernacular. He had the face of a white man, but he sounded like a black cat straight off the streets. Mississippi grew up with a few white friends in Alabama, who hung around Blacks so much, they adapted many of their ways and mannerisms, but never like what he just saw and heard. He was just about to respond to his request, when he got a closer look at them, and that patented broad smile came to his face. He thought "these fellas are not white at all, at least not all white".

Mississippi then responded, "No I'm cool, I'm just spectating today". Without hesitation, the older one introduced himself. "My name is Phil Gardner, and this is my brother, Howie". They both extended their hands, and while shaking their hands, Mississippi got an even closer look. "My friends call me Mississippi."

Ever since Mississippi came to New York, his social circle was cautiously small. He didn't drink, and his appetite for chasing females waned, thus narrowing his circle even more. People naturally were gravitated towards him, but for obvious reasons, he basically kept to himself. In the case of the Gardner Brothers, maybe for the sake of curiosity, he began hanging out with Phil and Howard Gardner.

They were born in upstate New York in a small town called Newburg. Their father was white and their mother, a very lighted-skin black woman. Their father was a career military man and he retired right before the start of World War II. His wife never traveled with her husband as most wives do. He chose not to subject her through the complications a black wife would bring in a very racist, segregated army. She gladly stayed at home, and raised their two sons.

Just before the United States chose to go to war, the two sons joined the army. It was an easy decision for them because their father planted that idea in their heads almost as soon as they came out of the womb. Their Caucasian looks, for some, would have been a clear ticket to pass for white and receive all the privileges on the *white side* of the armed forces. However, they loved their *colored mother* and their black heritage, and passing for white was the furthest thing on their minds. Phillip became an administrator in charge of procurements, and Howie became a truck driver. Like most black soldiers, they saw very little combat, and they were alright with that. In the beginning, they were stationed in England. Soon after D-Day, June 1944, they were transferred to France. After their first tour of duty was over, they immediately signed up for another four years. Their father was so proud of his two sons for signing up again, but their reasons had nothing to do with duty or country. As soon as the war began to turn for the Allies in Europe, and Hitler's troops could no longer stage offensive battles, those moments of peace became golden opportunities for the Black Market. In the midst of all the chaos and confusion, someone in charge of thousands of warehouses, and a few cooperative truck drivers, could do pretty well for themselves.

Phillip and his brother Howie sold everything from lady's stockings to T-bone steaks, and everything in between. They had the best of both sides of the color barrier. They could bargain with the black soldiers and cross the line, and do business with their white servicemen. It's needless to say that the white warehouses had far better quality of goods than the colored. When the war finally ended, and the shooting stopped, they made even more money. America had the task of helping Europe rebuild its infrastructure, and the Gardner Brothers lined their pockets.

When President Truman started the conversation about integrating the armed forces, Phil and Howard agreed, it was time to move on. They figured an integrated army would take the fun out of their exploits. Nonetheless, they still had one more year on their tour, so they doubled down on their larceny, and enjoyed some of the finest women Europe had to offer. It also demands mentioning that they fell in love with jazz music, and they saw and heard some of the greatest jazz musicians in the world. When money got tight and gigs were few in the United States, jazz artists found new life, and a welcome audience in Europe. When the time came for the Garner Brothers to say farewell to their European playground, they brought home boxes of jazz records and boxes of cash.

Mississippi was not too keen on jazz. In fact, his musical taste was not definitive at all. After hanging out with Phil and Howard, they opened his eyes and ears to what Phil would describe as "the greatest music ever created". Mississippi never talked about his business with his new buddies. He did invite them to his house on Sugar Hill, a few times. When he finally got the chance to see their dwellings he was impressed. It was an upscale hotel much like the Hoffman but further uptown towards the Bronx. Their suite was beautifully furnished, two-bedrooms, decent living and dining areas, and a balcony that provided a grand view of the New York skyline. Mississippi's analytical and calculating mind was puzzled by one observation. When he lived at the Hoffman, one look around his flat and you could see all the signs of permanency, but their resident looked very temporary, and they would soon reveal why.

Jake's pool hall was near capacity when Mississippi strolled through the doors. Phil had asked to meet him there after his business was done. Phil and Black Sam were shooting a casual game of nine ball in the far corner. Mississippi greeted and chatted with a few friends as he walked towards their table. Black Sam was loud and boisterous as always. "Mississippi, I'm glad to see you, cause this white boy is whipping my ass", he announced. They all laughed and Sam gladly went to the other side of the room. "Got a proposition for you my friend", Phil stated. "Follow me to my apartment, and I'll explain it there."

When Phillip and Howard Gardner were discharged from the army, finding jobs and getting married were not in their plans. They had accumulated enough money to live the way they were accustomed, while they figured out what their next move would be. The integration of the Armed Forces and other attempts to bring balance to the social and economic structure of the United States, had all the right intentions. However, they simply did not produce the desired results. In fact, America was more polarized than ever. The conversation about integration only angered the whites more, and black people merely shrugged their shoulders about the realization of equal rights. The Gardner Brothers saw all this as another opportunity to use their white skin and wits to take their earnings to an even higher level.

To pull this off, they would need the skills of an expert. They hired an aging make-up artist name Guiseppi. He worked on Broadway, and even did some of Hollywood's early movies. Guiseppi's skills were impeccable. He could make a bone white Caucasian look like a genuine Native Indian. He was also responsible for some of those early *black face* roles. For the Gardner Brothers, his job was going to be easy. They simply wanted to look white, and because of their genetic heritage, they were already halfway there. Guiseppi brought a couple of very good quality wigs. He then custom cut the hairpieces to fit their faces. He instructed them on applying just a little facial make-up, and the finishing product was astounding. Phil and Howie went to the Brooks Brothers Clothier and purchased 4 of the most expensive suits in the store. They put their suits on, along with their wigs and make-up, and if you didn't know them, one would think they were bankers.

At first they tried the smaller banks in the suburbs. They would simply deposit a substantial amount of cash in the targeted bank. The purpose was to get the bank manager to get to know and recognize them. Then a week or so later, enter the bank, approach that same manager, and quietly threaten him with a partially visible firearm, walk him over to the safe, and fill their briefcase up with cash. No one is ever alarmed, because a couple of "white cats" with expensive suits are simply not alarming.

They would return to the black neighborhood where they resided, as the police scowled and searched for two white bank robbers. The two brothers repeated this four times. Now it was time to go after the bigger fish, and they needed a third man.

"Why me?' Mississippi responded after listening to and visualizing their costumes and stories. "Is it because of my light skin", he sarcastically added. Phil always did most of the talking, in fact Mississippi can only recall a few times when the younger brother, Howard, said anything at all. "It's more to this than what the eye sees", Phil insisted. "I know a hundred cats that are light-skinned, but Mississippi, I chose to ask you because of your calculating abilities." Mississippi gave them a puzzling look. "Your policy business and your house on 112th Street are all risks, but very well planned and operated." This statement raised Mississippi's eyebrows. The fact that they knew about his enterprises, made him listen even more. However, as he listened to them, he could also hear Rico's voice in his head saying "all the money is not yours". Then with the same defiance that made him buy that train ticket to New York, rather than Chicago, he nodded his head in agreement with his new partners.

Mississippi was fitted with a hairpiece, a new suit, and a little extra make-up because of his darker complexion. Surprisingly, it went off as smooth as ever. So smooth, a month later, they repeated the job on the other side of Manhattan. Then without fanfare or notice, the Gardner Brothers packed their bags, and left town. They never mentioned where and Mississippi never asked.

His personal stash was now well over $150,000.00, and that thought brought that broad smile to his face once again. He was now faced with a dilemma.

Something like this may get back to Rico, or maybe he never knows, but he had too much respect for their relationship, so he decided to resign from the policy business. He never explained why, and Rico accepted his resignation and they remained close friends. He then poured extra time and energy into his business on 112th Street, and spent more time learning and playing the game of pool, that he has grown to truly love.

English Dan knew none these details of Mississippi's past, but the huge wad of cash indicated that he was some kind of hustler. Mississippi was conservatively dressed as always, with a springtime Italian knit shirt, and a pair of very expensive slacks. It was almost as if Dan was looking at himself, which brought a tiny smile. He didn't appear to be a boastful cat like his buddy Black Sam. However, every pool hustler has an ego, and there was nothing that indicated that Mississippi was any different. Dan's task was to find a way to stroke his ego, separate some of that wad of cash, and at the same time, make him feel good about it.

His young opponent, Scooter seemed happy just to be on the same table with Mississippi, even after losing five games to the tune of one hundred dollars.

"Must be one of his underlings" thought Dan. As Scooter respectfully shook Mississippi's hand, sighting the end of his uphill battle. Dan intervened, "Mr. Mississippi, couldn't help notice that you are a pretty good shooter, however, if you wanted to be better, you need to take that little hitch out of your stroke." "And who the hell are you?" "No disrespect, my name is English Dan and I wouldn't mind showing you how it's done, but the lesson is gonna cost you one hundred dollars a game", Dan whispered not to draw any undue attention from the crowd. This was not an attempt to show-up Mississippi, who immediately realized that and whispered back, "that's a bet". This wasn't some elaborate con game. Dan noticed that Mississippi loved the game and he also noticed that regardless of his street reputation, he had a touch of humility that would allow him to take on instructions. There was no better teacher than English Dan.

In the first game, his was masterful, perfect posture, smooth stroke, and Mississippi was impressed. The second game was no different, however, when Dan missed on the 5 ball, he gave his eager student a few pointers on how to attack the rest of the table. Dan would eventually win that game also. But

Mississippi played much better in the 3rd and 4th games. He knew he was way over his head, and the money didn't matter. It was a pleasure just to see Dan work the table. "I'm gonna beat you the next game", Miss said with a chuckle. As he bent over to rack the balls, there was a loud commotion at the front door.

Everyone in the pool hall turned in that direction. Ted Lattimore was off to the side of the entrance talking to Sonny the owner, when a tall older cat came through the door screaming and cursing. No one could determine who was the intended ire of this angry man, until the irate man bellowed, "Mississippi, how many times have I told you to stay away from my girls!" Now everyone turned in the direction of Mississippi, who kept racking the balls as if nothing had occurred. This made the well-dressed man even angrier, and he started to step towards Mississippi when Sonny calmly walked over to the gentleman, and whispered in his ear, "Tony, not in my place." Sonny did not tolerate any outside bullshit in his pool hall, and everyone in Harlem knew it. Pretty Tony's touch of amnesia quickly faded, and he patted his well-groomed processed hair as if to make sure it was still in place, and quietly turned, and exited through the door and down the stairs.

Everyone except Sonny and Mississippi blew a sigh of relief and continued their games. Pretty Tony was an aging pimp who was known to use his straight razor on his girls, and anyone else who got in his way. Sonny, who was now over at Mississippi's table, wasn't fazed by Tony's reputation or anyone else's. Sonny's calm demeanor could turn lethal in a heartbeat and everyone from the local gangsters to the regular working folks, respected him. "Sonny, I do apologize for that disturbance" Mississippi insisted. "My friend Tony doesn't realize that the game is over" he said with a broad smile. Over the last two years Tony's girls had grown tired of his violence and his old ways. Mississippi and a few of the younger cats offered women more of a cut of the proceeds and a safer working environment. This was a sure fire recipe for Pretty Tony's decline. Sonny was not concerned with any of those details, however, he liked Mississippi and his apology was more than enough.

"Dan, I must also apologize to you, wouldn't want you to leave our fine city with the wrong impression", he said with slight laugh. "Hey Ted", Sonny yelled from across the room, "Is this your young sharp shooter you've been telling me about?" Ted came over to the table and his broad grin was enough of an answer. "Let me introduce Mr. English Dan to you fellas." No need, we've already met. Mississippi added, "While you two were catching up on old times, Dan has been showing me some of the finest pool shooting I've ever seen. I'd like to continue, but I've gotta talk to my colleague, Pretty Tony before he has a heart attack". "Hold on Miss, Sonny interrupted, "Is he better than Little Augie?" The question made Mississippi come to a screeching stop. "Ain't seen him in a while, but that's a damn good question. I'll tell you what" Miss continued, "I'd love to see them two go at it." "Well if we can convince these two gentlemen to come back tomorrow, I'll see if I can arrange that" Sonny replied. The crowd loved a good pool match. It's good for the game and most of all, it's good for business. Dan had no fear of any pool shooter, but he would rather feed on the lesser talents, than go up against the best in the house. On the other hand, Ted's face lit up like a light bulb. "We'll be here Sonny."

"How did we do today," Ted asked as they drove to their Manhattan Hotel. "I won one hundred from big mouth Sam and another two from a couple other cats." "I did four hundred from Mississippi and would've won more if we weren't disturbed, Dan said in a disappointing tone." 'Yeah I know but this is Harlem", Ted replied, "That would be considered a quiet night up here, that's why I bring along my little companion. Ain't looking for trouble, but if it comes along don't wanna be unprepared." So far the trip had been a success. They won twelve hundred in Boston and another seven in Harlem and were experiencing something they could talk about for years to come. Ted got the chance to see some of his old acquaintances and the young English Dan having settled down, was shooting some of the finest pool he has ever shot. "Tell me a little bit about this cat, Little Augie", Dan commanded. Dan always liked to know a little about his opponent. "Don't know much about his personal life, Ted answered and I never saw him shoot but word on the streets, says he became so good, he couldn't get a game anywhere in Harlem, his finances got so bad he had to go get a regular job." Dan looked at Ted as they got on the elevator with a puzzling look. "So why in the hell would we go after a cat like this, he can't be beat and if he's a working stiff, he doesn't have much money to lose." Ted became a little irritated with that statement, mostly because Dan was right. However, Ted Lattimore had only one thing on his mind, when he walked into a pool hall. That was to beat the best shooter in the house, and if he couldn't do it, he would empty his pockets trying. The only thing English Dan had on his mind when he walked into a pool hall, is to be the one walking out with the cash.

CHAPTER 12

The Second Coming of Little Augie

———

"LITTLE AUGIE" WAS BORN ARTHUR Bennett on New Year's Day in 1926, to loving, but very poor parents in Harlem. They called this era the "Roaring Twenties", but that description was limited to club owners and bootleggers. The rest of America, especially black folk struggled and the Great Depression would soon make times even harder. Baby Arthur brought a much needed touch of joy to the Bennetts. Leon worked as a baggage handler at the train station and his beautiful wife, Dora, was a hardworking domestic on the far side of town. Yes, times were very tough but they had each other and they were grateful, in a world where gratitude was lost in the pursuit of unattainable riches. When the stock market crashed in 1929, the world around them seemed to fall apart, but the Bennetts, like most Negroes, were used to hard times and they persevered.

One of Arthur's childhood friends had a bad speech impediment, and he had a terrible time pronouncing Arthur's name. Every time he said it, it came out "Augur" and eventually everyone began to call him "Augie". By the time he reached eight-years old, it was apparent that he was going be short in height and the nickname "Little Augie" stuck like glue. Leon was extremely fond of his son. Every chance, in his already demanding schedule, he spent time with Little Augie. There simply was not much cash on hand, so they sought out the more quaint activities like the park, the playground and the zoo. It was 1934 and it may have been recorded as the most bleak era in America's history, but the Bennetts always chose a more optimistic outlook, and the tight bond of their tiny family could withstand anything that crossed their threshold.

Leon rose at the crack of dawn and walked ten blocks to the trolley, as he did every day. Upon arriving at the train station, he punched his time card and began to change into his uniform. He worked the New York to Boston train in the morning and the

Boston to Washington DC train in the afternoons. The Washington portion of his day brought the most tips. The politicians and their aides were very generous. As he climbed the stairs to the platform, an extremely sharp pain struck the center of his chest. He grabbed the railing hoping the pain would subside, but another sharp pain caused him to sit down on the steps. One of his co-workers ran to his aid, while another ran to the foreman's office. They called for an ambulance, but when the paramedics arrived at the hospital, they pronounced Leon Bennett dead of an apparent massive heart attack.

It was nearly noon before the tragic news of his death came back to the foreman at the station. The foreman was now faced with the dubious task of contacting his wife. The Bennett's did not have a telephone, in fact very few people did. They used a telephone booth across the street from their apartment building. The foreman thought about asking one of Leon's co-workers to travel to Harlem and give his family the bad news, but he had a lot of respect for Leon, and chose to do it himself after his shift was over.

When Leon did not arrive home at his normal time of 6:30pm, Dora never gave it a thought of concern. It was not uncommon for her husband to do extra work, and the trains were sometimes delayed as well. She began to prepare her dinner, as Little Augie played in the hallway with a few of his friends. When the door at the stairway opened, the first thing Little Augie saw was a middle-aged white man, catching his breath after climbing four flights to the fourth floor. The next thing he saw was the railroad insignia on the left side of his jacket. That got Arthur's attention because he saw it before on his father's uniform. The stranger then openly asked the boys, "any of you boys know which one is Apartment D?" Before any of them responded, they all looked in Little Augie's direction, who blurted out "that's my apartment!"

This saddened the foreman even more and he slowly walked towards the door of Apartment D. Dora thought it was her son wanting a snack, but when she opened the door and saw that same insignia, it made her freeze for a split second. The foreman began to tell the tragic tale and her instinctive denial literally blocked out the context of his story. The thought of her husband not coming home again was too much to digest. The foreman then gave her a slight hug and an envelope of cash the workers donated and he was gone.

Dora was too stunned to cry. Her first thought was "how can I tell my son his father will never come home again." The sad news left Little Augie with a blank expression on his face. He didn't even shed a tear at the funeral. When Dora had to take on another job, this left Arthur unsupervised for hours every day. The streets became his playground and there probably were no tougher neighborhoods in the entire world than those dark gritty streets of Harlem. As Arthur grew older, the only thing that grew faster was that anger in his heart and there was nothing his beloved mother could do to ease his pain. His small statue made him a welcoming target for the local bullies. But they all soon realized Little Augie was not an "easy win". The fights increased and the school work disappeared. Dora heard about a school that recently opened in 1933.

It started out as one of those social experiments. The cities across the country was experiencing some of the hardest times in its brief history. There were thousands of angry, displaced and confused young boy's desperately trying to make sense of their inherited situation. The New York State Training School for boys in Warwick, New York was a ray of hope for the children and the parents as well.

The mission was simple, take hundreds of young men out of their violent and dysfunctional environments, give them some basic, elementary education, coupled with vocational and farming skills and allow them to grow into productive adults. The school had operated with a mediocre rate of success since it was established. Dora watched helplessly, as her once cheerful eight-year old son, turned into this irate, contemptuous teenager. She was willing to try anything.

The Warwick School, as it eventually became known as, was 60 miles outside of New York City in Orange County. Living cottages sat on hundreds of acres. These acres also contained farmland which allowed the facility to plant their own food and raise their livestock. Counselors were assigned specific cottages and it was their job to educate, orientate, and hopefully point these young men in the right direction.

They told Dora the school would do everything possible to help Arthur grow into a positive young man. However, the only thing that grew on Little Augie was the *chip* that was already on his shoulder when he first arrived. His counselor, Mr. Levin tried dutifully to get him to interact with the other boys.

Arthur felt betrayed by his mother and cheated by the untimely death of his father. He went to his classes and performed his mandatory chores, but everything was done with a permanent scowl on his face.

After about a year in Warwick, a generous benefactor made a donation that would literally change Arthur's life. That donation was two brand new pool tables. Mr. Levin was a fairly good player and he taught the boys the basic pool shooting skills. Some of the young men enjoyed the new tables, but Little Augie was captivated by the game. Whenever he got a chance, he was shooting pool. While the other boys were in the yard playing baseball, Little Augie was playing pool. Mr. Levin began to seek out competition to sharpen Augie's skills and he would never disappoint. He was so proud of his student, he brought an adult pool hustler from Bensonhurst to the school and Little Augie never gave him a chance to shoot.

Dora came for a visit and burst into tears to see her son smile. Little Augie still had that scowl but smiling was not as difficult anymore. On New Year's Day 1944, Arthur turned 18. In the spring of that same year, Little Augie graduated from Warwick. They gave him a certificate in carpentry, and if they were giving out diplomas for pool shooting, Little Augie would have received a Masters.

About six months before Arthur graduated, his mom had grown tired of Harlem and moved to Danville Virginia, her birth place. She longed for a more-simple lifestyle and her parents were delighted with her decision. She hoped Arthur would join her, but Little Augie loved Harlem and chose to stay. He found a job as a porter not too far from the train station where his beloved father worked. Whenever he had any spare time, Little Augie was in the pool halls. He had no idea how valuable were his newly acquired skills.

He played for nickels and dimes and mostly for the love of the game. He frequented the same two or three pool halls, and little did he know, he aroused the interest of a certain individual.

This curious and watchful pair of eyes belong to a mid-level numbers banker. He had a good eye for special talent. He had not seen a young shooter with the skills of Arthur and he saw many excellent pool shooters. Never speaking a word, he watched Little Augie for over a month. The only flaw he saw in his game was that, this young man can get very angry, real fast.

In all the major cities all across the country, pool hustling was rapidly becoming extremely popular. New York's five boroughs had hundreds of pool halls and they were filled with some of the most prolific shooters in the land. These skillful artisans had ever present bulging pool shooters egos, along with bulging pockets. This combination proved to be explosive and the games popularity did just that. The timing could not have been more perfect. It was time for the pool hustlers of the world to witness the likes of *Little Augie.*

Arthur emerged from the subway and headed straight for Jake's Pool Hall off of Lennox Avenue. He still had his work uniform on. As he approached the entrance, he noticed a well-dressed cat standing near the door. "Arthur, can I speak to you for a few ticks?" the number banker asked. Little Augie had seen this gentleman around but never bothered to acquaint himself. "Sure, what's up?" he answered. Arthur never got a chance to shoot any pool that night. The numbers man whisked him away in a shiny automobile and when the night was over, the two of them agreed to a 40/60 *stake horse* deal. The conversation went so well, Little Augie knew he had something special when he left Warwick, but after talking to the well-dressed stranger, and listening to his well-planned strategy, the decision was easy.

Ten years older than Arthur, he polished his appearance and his game. He even showed him how to control his temper. This factor really left a lasting impression on Little Augie. The stranger said things that made him smile. He only knew two men in his life that was able to do that, Mr. Levin at Warwick, and his father. That gifted stranger was Sonny Carson.

Sonny had two major factors in his favor. The first was that his money was long enough to go after the heavy bettors. Sonny was only a mid-level banker, but he was a good business man. Second, no one outside of a few pool halls in Harlem knew who Little Augie was. Sonny knew it only just a matter of time for Little Augie's reputation to grow. It was imperative that they hit the circuit of halls, hard and fast. Sonny decided to run through Harlem first. It was decent money in Harlem, but not what Sonny was aiming for. This would give Little Augie a chance to loosen up and also give Sonny a chance to see *his horse* in real action. It was a breeze as Little Augie ran up against some real sharp shooters. Sonny was impressed, so much he went straight after the heavy bettors when he reached the Bronx. The colored side of Brooklyn was no different. However, Sonny had to use his mob connections to venture to the white side of Bedford Stuyvesant. Under the protection of a local mob lieutenant, Sonny and Little Augie went into a hall filled with white cats. Half of them were connected and the rest were some of the finest pool shooters this side of the Hudson. After it was over, Sonny and Little Augie left the hall with close to ten thousand dollars. They were amazed at Augie's talent and on the surface there were no hard feelings, but Sonny decided to quit early before their welcome wore out. In a daring move a week later, they crossed the line and went to Bensonhurst, the heavily populated Jewish neighborhood. There was no mob protection, but Sonny knew the pool hall owner and he gave them his blessings. When the two of them crossed the threshold, all heads turned, but when Sol, the owner, shook Sonny's hand, the crowd quieted down. As Little Augie removed his jacket, he saw the same Jewish pool hustler Mr. Levin brought to Warwick. At first Augie thought Ira was going to blow his cover but the gentleman just nodded at Augie and continued his game. Ira knew how good Augie was but he didn't want to miss this himself. In fact, once Augie started playing, he put his cue stick in the rack and got a front row position. Augie was dazzling and Ira, his Jewish acquaintance, just smiled as shooter after shooter tried to beat the young Mr. Arthur Bennett. When the smoke cleared, Sonny tipped the helper twenty dollars, and gave Sol, the owner, one hundred dollars as a gesture of appreciation. When they were in the privacy of their car, Sonny counted a total of twenty-one hundred dollars, and once again he made Little Augie smile.

The formula for their success was simple. Augie provided the raw and unbeatable talent, while Sonny's job was to insure a safe venue and equally as important, stroke these immense egos and keep them thinking they could one day beat Little Augie. However, Sonny's most important task was to keep Arthur Bennett's anger in check.

For over six months, every night they went home smiling. Sonny taught Augie everything he knew. He also knew that the more Little Augie learned, the more confident he would become. This confidence would spawn the need for independence. Sonny knew it was just a matter of time before Arthur

Bennett would ask to go on his own. Anticipating this day would soon come, Sonny, the excellent businessman, saved nearly all of his winnings. Part of those winnings he used to expand his numbers bank, and the rest would go to something he had his eye on for a long time, his own pool hall.

Little Augie Bennett received his mentor's blessing and suddenly he was on his own. He did not have the connections Sonny had, so he had to limit his circle of pool halls. At first, Augie did well. It was strange when people saw him alone, and it annoyed him a little because everyone kept asking for Sonny. When his reputation began to scare potential bettors, his winnings began to dwindle. Irritated by all of this, Little Augie's anger began to slowly creep back and Sonny was not around to quell it. Pool is a game of immense concentration. The great shooters make it look easy, but it takes a cool and calm individual to succeed. The more savvy shooters also look for an opponent's weakness, and as soon as a few of the heavy bettors exposed Augie's fragile side, they came after him. They realized that if you can get under his skin and arouse that once dormant anger, he was not so invincible after all. Arthur Bennett ran into a couple of buzz saws and that once confident yet arrogant personae disappeared. He was not accustomed to losing and decided that his pool days were over. At the tender age of 21, three years since he left Warwick, Little Augie found a job with the city's sanitation department and no one saw much of him again.

Sonny Carson parlayed his earnings and convinced an aging Jacob Epstein into leasing Jakes Pool Hall. That was five years ago, in 1947. Upon hearing about the young phenom, English Dan, it brought back fond memories of his former partner. Sonny thought about Mississippi's statement of putting the two together and his calculating business mind began to churn. It's true, Little Augie had not come around for years, however, finding him would be no problem for Sonny. A few years after leaving the pool scene, Arthur Bennett married Sonny's younger sister and was raising a family on the other side of town.

CHAPTER 13

The Showdown

———

NIGGER CHRISTMAS WAS A TERM used in the 1920's and 30's. It described a particular day of the week and the enchanting "spell of excitement" it had on Black Folk. There is probably no place in the entire world more exciting than a *Friday Night in Harlem*. The streets were alive and it was still early. Dan had convinced Ted to get there early, and work on some of the easier money. As the shiny Oldsmobile coasted down the street, Dan's senses revisited the sights and sounds of New York. It was even more mesmerizing than the day before.

"Wow", Dan whispered, "you would think today was Christmas or something". Ted laughed and replied, "It is." They methodically removed their cue cases and the five hundred dollars of betting cash from the trunk and headed for Sonny's. Dan noticed a certain unusual air of excitement in Ted as they climbed the stairs. Ted's anxiousness made Dan even calmer. He had to remind himself, it was just another Friday night in a pool hall. However, when they opened the door, the reality hit them. Yes, it was Friday, but it wasn't just another pool hall.

The place was electric and it was only three o'clock. It was as if Sonny had hung a sign outside advertising the "Return of Little Augie Bennett". There were people inside who haven't been in the pool hall for years, and the conversation was all about Little Augie and the stranger named English Dan. Black Sam was dressed up in his usual dazzling outfit talking to Sonny in the corner. Ted headed in that direction but Dan chose not to go that way. It would probably be another two hours before Augie would show up and it was important for Dan to remain that unknown stranger. If the shooters knew he was the mysterious man in question, they wouldn't come within 10 feet of him. In hopes of making a few bucks, he waved to Sonny and made his way through the throngs of spectators and put a nickel in the coke machine, and focused his attention on two middle-aged cats playing *9 Ball*.

"What time is your man gonna show?" Ted asked while shaking Sonny's hand. Sonny just smiled, he was enjoying this moment. He told a few people that Little Augie would make a return to the pool hall on Friday and the word spread like brush fire. There were still quite a few cats who appreciated the "fine science of billiards", and the turnout was a reflection of that fact.

"You'd better be careful whatcha asking for my friend", Sonny responded in a cynical tone. "Just how good is he?" snapped Ted. "Well a few years ago I personally saw him run three *8 Ball* racks without missing a single shot. That's how good he is. As a matter of fact, what year was that Sam? 1949, 50?" Sam gave Sonny a very peculiar look and shouted, "How in the hell would I know something like that!" "You should know because he ran those racks against you." Everyone in the corner who was within earshot of that exchange roared in a hearty laugh with Black Sam laughing the loudest. Ted had been hearing stories about Arthur Bennett since his first trips to Harlem. These stories only intensified Ted's desire to play and hopefully beat Little Augie.

In spite of all the excitement about the second coming of Little Augie, there were still three games in progress. One table had one young boy taking advantage of Joey Diamond, an older guy with very thick eye glasses. Joey was an excellent shooter in his day, but the sugar began to gradually take away his eyesight. He loved the game so much, he said, "I'll keep shooting until I'm blind." The second table was occupied by two cats who look like they were just killing time, waiting for the main attraction. However, the third table donned two very well dressed middle-aged gentlemen playing nine ball for twenty bucks a game. The brown skinned taller fella was Jimmy Long, who ran a very large number bank on the top side of Harlem. The other expensively dressed cat was Rico Alvarez. His number bank was twice as big that engulfed all of Spanish Harlem. Dan put another nickel in the coke machine, and as he sipped on the soda, he contemplated his dilemma. These two distinguished cats had money longer than train smoke, so waiting for one of them to tap out wasn't feasible. The other side of the problem was time. Little Augie would be strolling through the door in a couple of hours. As Dan sized up the two, he couldn't help notice the quality of their attire. Jimmy had on a pair spring wool slacks tailor made to fit and the short sleeved

Italian knit shirt that looked like they stitched it on him. Rico's silk and wool pants were the finest Dan had ever seen and the alligator shoes were simply *untouchable*. When Rico made a very difficult shot on the nine ball, the break in the action gave Dan a small window of opportunity. "Couldn't help notice that you two fellas were playing the only serious game in the joint". Dan politely intervened and "I was wondering if, I could get in on a game or two?" As Dan grabbed the rack, he also reached in his pocket and pulled out his huge wad of cash. "With no disrespect, I'll play for whatever we can agree." Dan paused for a reaction and then added, "that's a mighty fine pair of skins you are wearing my man and the only place in the world that you could find them is New York and London." Dan's insight on the finest clothes paid off. Rico nodded his head with approval. The two then gave Dan the *once over*, a head to toe look sizing up his clothes and intentions. Dan as usual was dressed to the *nines* and his un-alarming personae made the two number bankers feel relaxed. "Why not?" Jimmy Long responded. What's your name young man?" English Dan hesitated for a second and answered. "Danny, they call me Danny." He began to rack the nine balls and before they could process his response. He asked, "How does fifty a game sound!" Having stroked their egos and gave them the utmost respect, Rico, the number banker who ran all of Spanish Harlem, replied, "Bet". English Dan quietly won the first three games. Money was not an issue for these two gentlemen so the fact of Dan winning three games never bothered them. They were, as all others were, simply enjoying the fine pool shooting of English Dan.

As Dan smoothly won the fourth game, the crowd continued to flow in and now the place was almost at maximum capacity. They were elbow to elbow, and the chatter of Little Augie was as loud as ever. Dan's table was near the front door and as he chalked up his cue stick with his back to the door, Sonny's Pool Hall got even louder. "English Dan, my man!" The loud entrance startled Dan and what he saw when he turned around, it was Mississippi decked out in a two-piece vine, with two very fine women one on each arm. His entrance got the attention of the rest of the crowd, and anyone who didn't know who the tall stranger was before, they surely knew now. Mississippi shook Dan's hand, and walked over to Rico and gave him a handshake and embrace. When Mississippi first arrived in New York, ten years ago, it was Rico who looked out for him and they have been close friends ever since. "Rico, you cats know who this is?" as he put his arm around Dan's shoulder. What y'all playing for? Fifty, a hundred a game? Next question, how many games have you won?" Rico and Jimmy just looked at each other and smiled. "That's what I thought", continued Mississippi. "I'm gonna save you two fellas some money and introduce Mr. English Dan to these two lovely ladies. You both can thank me later." The popularity of Mississippi and the anxiousness to meet English Dan had the crowd hanging on his every word. This entertaining exchange brought a warm round of laughter from the crowd and Rico was the first to walk over to Dan and shake his hand. "That was some of the best pool shooting I've seen in a long time young man. If I was a betting man, I'd have to put my money on you", he said sarcastically. Dan respectfully nodded and also shook Jimmy's hand and a few of the other men in the crowd. Mississippi then swept him away and Dan found himself in the company of two of the most beautiful women he had ever seen. On the other side of the pool hall, Ted Lattimore was beaming with delight and appreciation over the attention his young phenom was getting. Sonny looked at his watch and sported a broad grin. He knew it was just a matter of time before Arthur Bennett would show.

Life after his pool shooting run was very good for Little Augie. Sonny's sister, Lisa was almost a perfect match for hm. Her calm, serene resolve was therapeutic for the angry, edgy Arthur Bennett. After their second child, he became the ideal husband and adoring father and that gritty young man with the permanent scowl on his face, cease to exist. He never shot pool again and unlike some pool hustlers who removed themselves from the game, there wasn't this burning desire to return. So when Sonny came by late Thursday with the offer to shoot again, he almost turned him down. However, the moment he agreed to show up, that flame that made him one of Harlem's most prolific pool shooters, began to burn in his gut once again.

As Little Augie came out of the 125th Street subway entrance, a touch of excitement he had not felt in a long time overcame him. "It's been a long time" he said to himself, "I hope I still got it?" The minute he went through the door, the crowd went crazy and it wasn't until that moment, did Arthur Bennett realize how much he missed the game. Augie never became that savvy pool hustler. He was just one helluva pool shooter and every single person in the room wondered "if he still had it". They all knew that if he does still have it, they were in for quite a show.

Sonny waded through the crowd and gave his brother-in-law a big hug. Sonny was a very astute businessman. The minute he heard about the sharp shooting of English Dan, he began to formulate a plan to bring Arthur Bennett out of retirement. Little Augie left a lot of good pool hustlers with empty pockets, so when they heard about his return, they would show up to get another glimpse of his greatness. Sonny also was hoping they would show with bulging pockets, and that lingering bitter taste of defeat, still gnawing in their gut.

"Alright, now all of you cats just settle down for a moment," Sonny bellowed as Arthur continued to greet all of his well-wishers. "Most of y'all know Little Augie and those who don't know him will sure get the chance to meet him soon." Sonny continued as he smiled and glanced over at Ted and English Dan. "Now a lot of y'all think my man is rusty after that long absence and that very well may be, but the question is how much are you willing to put up to find out?" Sonny then reached into his pocket and pulled out a tremendous wad of cash and held it up for all to see. "My partner and I are taking all bets from a sawbuck for the faint at heart", Sonny paused and smiled. "And up to a grand for the more courageous." The crowd went into a murmuring frenzy. Sonny then motioned to his employee, Johnny Boy to clean off the center table. It wasn't as fancy as Chick's center table, but it was adequate. Ted Lattimore methodically began to assemble his cue stick. English Dan with his cue stick resting on his shoulder, began to size up Little Augie. The rest of the crowd positioned themselves for a good place to witness what might very well be, some of the best pool shooting they may ever see.

Uptown Joe grabbed a cue stick off the rack and shouted "I want him first." Joe was an excellent shooter, but like many hustlers, he was forced to get a regular job. However, when he was in the game, Little Augie used to *own* him. His pockets weren't bulging, but that bitter taste of defeat was as present as ever. "A double sawbuck a game" he proudly blurted. For most cats in the hall, twenty bucks wasn't that much, but it was still 1952 and twenty dollars was a half of a paycheck for Uptown Joe. They volleyed for the rights to break and Little Augie won. The entire crowd held its breath as Augie broke. The six ball fell, and the rust showed itself early, as he missed a relatively easy shot on the one ball. Joe's confidence swelled up and he ran the rest of the table and won the game. The next game was not much different, and Uptown Joe won again. As the crowd looked on in amazement, Joe walked over to Augie, shook his hand and then he walked over to the rack, replaced the stick and collected his second twenty-dollar bet from Sonny. Since leaving the game, Uptown had become more practical about money. The two wins helped mend his tattered ego, and it took him all of twenty minutes, to win an entire week's pay.

Ted Latimore tried to get to the table upon Joe's sudden departure, but Ace Harmon, a first cousin of Harlem gangster, Bumpy Johnson, slammed his hand on the table and said "y'all ready to shoot for some real money? One hundred dollars a game, Sonny!" This demand got everyone's attention, and Sonny just smiled. Many cats in the hall wondered if Augie was really that rusty, and some even wondered if it was all a ruse to get bigger bettors to surface. Ace won the volley, and with precision he began to drop balls.

Sonny and Little Augie could do nothing but watch. After running the entire table, he began to talk trash. "Sonny, you must think we're scared of Augie. You might as well get ready to give me all that money in your pocket." Sonny counted out one hundred dollars and placed it on the table as Ace Harmon continued. "What some of y'all don't know is that I'm the one who sent Little Augie into retirement."

Augie didn't respond because it was true. After going on his own, Augie lost nearly five hundred dollars to Ace, and it broke his bank and his spirit. "You gonna shoot pool, or you gonna shoot off your mouth", Augie said with an angry tone. The crowd let out a small burst of laughter. People tend to forget how angry he was with his newly discovered serenity. Sonny remembered all too well. It's been a long time since Arthur Bennett had to unleash that anger. His new found domestic tranquility allowed many to forget that side of him. However, Sonny would never forget, for it was him who showed Little Augie how to redirect his ire and focus on the game. "Don't let this sucker get under your skin Augie", Sonny demanded, "Send this nigger home broke". Ace went on to win the next two games. But the rust on Little Augie's game began to disappear.

Dan was standing next to Mississippi intently taking in all this activity. His keen eye made him notice that even though Mr. Bennett lost that third game, all that nervous energy he started with, had passed. Dan also noticed a certain calmness in Augie as the fourth game began. The relentless trash talking continued. "We can do this all night long" as he broke. When no balls fell, Arthur Bennett went to work. He showed the crowd what they came to see. As he walked around the table to survey his shot selection, the room was deafly quiet. Then the balls began to fall, and when he sized up the ninth and final ball, a tiny smile appeared on his face. After winning his first game, he loosened up. There was an air of confidence around him now and after the third straight win, Ace' s trash talking got even louder. However, Little Augie would not be deterred, and by the fifth win, he had the crowd in complete awe. He was pocketing some of the most difficult shots anyone had ever witnessed. When Ace lost his eighth game, he wanted to quit but his extra-large ego would not allow him to. And just like Sonny demanded earlier, Arthur Bennett sent him home broke. Ace Harmon silently slipped away after losing one thousand dollars.

After that extraordinary display, there was no one in the crowd that wondered if Augie sill had it. It's also fair to say that not too many were anxious to put up their money to find out. However, Ted Lattimore waited for his chance. Although he just saw some of the finest pool shooting in his life, Ted stepped up without blinking. He didn't come here to watch. "We can keep it at a hundred a game Sonny". Ted's pool game was just above average and no one knew that better than Dan. Ted won the volley and broke and the six and four balls fell. The only problem was that the one ball was in a bad spot. The proper move would be to pass upon trying for the one, and put the cue ball in a place that put Augie at a disadvantage. However, Ted tried to make the nearly impossible shot on the one, and opened up the rest of table. Augie calmly ran the table, as English Dan shook his head with despair. Ted took advantage of a rare mistake by Little Augie, and won the second game. The joy and confidence from that win was short lived, as Augie got very serious and won the next five games, exhausting Ted's betting cash. Ted thought about going to his trunk for more, but he knew he was way over his head. As he walked over to shake Arthur Bennett's hand, Dan's rule, not to take more than 500 hundred dollars into any pool hall, now seemed like a very good idea.

The pool hall was still murmuring about some of the fantastic shots they just saw. Little Augie stood silently waiting for his next opponent. Sonny was standing nearby sporting a very wide grin. He nodded his head in the direction of English Dan, and Mississippi on the other side of the table. By now everyone knew who English Dan was, and why he was there. They all had just witnessed how great Little Augie was on the green felt table. Their curiosity was now on the tall, well dressed stranger. Common sense told Dan to take his couple hundred of dollars he won from Rico, and call it a night. This is not the first time he has ever run into a sharp shooter little Arthur Bennett, and it wouldn't be the first time he chose to walk away with his money still intact. However, his competitive spirit and the look of anticipation everyone had on their faces demanded that he do otherwise.

Even more important than all that, there was something Dan saw in Ted's only victory. In order to be an excellent pool shooter, you must have perfect shooting posture, and above that, good eyesight. When fatigue sets in, your posture and eyesight fades.

A well-conditioned pool hustler can shoot pool for more than eight hours, go home take a shower, have a meal, return and shoot for eight more. Augie had not shot pool for more than four years. He has already shot more than twenty games over the last four hours, and they were not easy games. In that one lost to Ted Lattimore, Dan saw Augie's posture change, and he missed a rather easy shot. No one else may have picked that up, but the long endless nights Dan has spent in pool halls, allowed him to recognize these things. The most important factor now is how to turn this information into cash.

'Two hundred a game", Dan announced. The crowd went into frenzy, trying to reposition themselves for a better view, and also for the first time tonight, the side bettors emerged. Many of them wanted to bet on Little Augie, but Mississippi already confident in the skills of English Dan, decided to take on all bets. Dan won the volley and the entire hall went silent as Dan broke the rack of nine. The balls scattered and the number two ball fell as did the number six ball. Then the only stripped ball in the rack, the number nine ball slowly crept to the corner pocket and stopped one inch from falling. The crowd let out a sighing gasp, and Ted Lattimore's smile returned to his face. The only problem with not pocketing the nine ball, is that Dan was left with only five pockets to work with. The other side of the problem was the one ball was in a very difficult position. The only shot Dan had was the one cushion bank shot. English Dan didn't hesitate, he lined up his cue stick and pocketed the one ball and then proceeded to smoothly run the rest of the table. Harlem's finest could do nothing, but watch as Sonny forked over the two hundred dollars.

Little Augie got a chance to shoot in the second game, but missed a difficult shot on the two ball, and Dan pocketed another two hundred dollars. On the third game, Arthur Bennett missed on the eight ball, and blew a chance to win. His fatigue was now a little more apparent, and Sonny as well as the side bettors began to take notice. Everyone in the room could sense the shift in momentum, and Dan was all business. He didn't crack a smile, nor did he play to the crowd. In the fourth game, Little Augie's frustration turned into anger as Sonny's smile, and confidence began to disappear. He reluctantly counted out another two hundred dollar wage. Augie had ample enough opportunities to win that game also, but couldn't make the necessary shots.

The air seemed to leave the room, and the celebratory atmosphere that had everyone smiling four hours ago, was gone. Only the stale cigarette smoke, and the collective broodiness hung like a dark cloud over the room. Even Mississippi and Black Sam, who were initially betting against Arthur, were not so thrilled at the sight of their native son being thrashed by the well-dressed stranger.

Dan chalked up the tip of his cue stick as Jimmy Boy racked the balls. He positioned the cue ball and took aim. He propelled the white cue ball into the pile and this time only one ball fell, the nine ball. It was a dagger like blow to Little Augie. All he could do was shake his head. The rest of the crowd was perplexed. The only one that was smiling was Ted Lattimore. As Sonny reached into his pocket once again, Dan began to disassemble his cue stick. He made his way across the room and gave Little Augie a hearty handshake, and then he walked over to Sonny and collected his wage. "Your horse is tired my friend. His pride and your deep pockets may not be ready to admit that. I tell yah what, I'll return to your fine establishment and we can continue this at another time." He walked back over to Little Augie, "Mr. Bennett, you shoot a helluva game, go home get some rest, and maybe in the very near future we can do this again." He then waved to the crowd and Mississippi started to applaud and then everyone else joined in. it was a gracious, and classy move and no one was more grateful than Arthur Bennett.

Dan took Little Augie's hand and raised it up in the air and the crowd applauded even louder. Arthur had been up since five in the morning. He was very thankful for Sonny's invitation, and even more thankful for his confidence. Sonny still managed to win five hundred dollars the 60/40 split gave Little Augie two hundred dollars. That was still over a month's wages in 1952. Arthur then said a few good byes, and quietly slipped out the door. It was great seeing some old friends and opponents, but Little Augie longed for the peace, and quiet of his family. As he watched Little Augie pass through the door, Sonny pondered a repeat match with English Dan, and a well-rested Arthur Bennett. The thought brought a smile back to Sonny's face, but that match would never become a reality, because that night would be the last night his brother-in-law would ever shoot pool again.

The mood in the hall had everyone very appreciative of the competition they had just witnessed.

They showered Dan with accolades, and handshakes. However, one person in Sonny's Pool Hall was not that festive. Ted Lattimore stood on the other side of the room disassembling and putting away his cue stick. His face wore a somber look of disappointment, and anger. The room was still fairly crowded and no one paid him much attention. English Dan had to pass him on the way to the soda machine, and he too paid him no attention. Dan knew what that frown on his face meant, but did not want to spoil his moment and besides, "I'll hear about it on the way back to the hotel" he thought.

"Mr. English Dan! You did not disappoint me", Mississippi said. "That was some of the best pool I've seen a long time. Hey Sonny we need to find a way to keep this young fella in town for a few." Sonny replied, "He's right Dan, there's a heap of pool halls in New York. It would be nice if I could convince you to stick around. I could put you up in one of my apartments." "I appreciate the offer fellas, but me and my man Ted, we gonna head on down to Baltimore in the morning." Dan shook a few hands and followed Ted out the door and down the stairs.

As soon as Ted reached the streets, he exploded into a tyrannical verbiage. "What the fuck were you thinking about Dan, why did you let them off of the hook?" He went on and on until Dan interrupted, "Ted you are a brilliant cat, and have a wealth of knowledge. You have been places, and seen things, I may never see in my lifetime. But if there's one thing I know, and that's pool." Dan paused to let what he just said soak in a little. Dan continued in a tone just above a whisper, "There's a whole lot more to pool than just hitting the balls and making the pockets. You must find a kink in the armor of your opponent, and try to use it against him. Little Augie had not played pool for years. He wasn't conditioned for the type of run Sonny was asking him to do. Knowing this, when you got on the table, you should have lessened the bet to fifty bucks and stretched out your cash and your chances of him getting tired. However, your ego would not allow you to see that." Dan had his undivided attention now. "When it was my turn, I immediately doubled the bet to two hundred. By that time, he was exhausted. I was tempted to bet five hundred a game but I didn't want to wake him up. He may have gotten a second wind and sent us all home broke." Ted tried to fight back a smile, but he couldn't. "Besides", Dan concluded, "sometimes it's good to let your opponent leave with a bet still in his pocket, but only sometimes. Sonny made a few bucks, and Little Augie went home with a few."

Ted's demeanor became amicable again, and Dan put his arm around his shoulder as they walked towards the car. "Besides those five games allowed us to walk away with the five hundred you quickly lost, and another five for our stash." Ted frowned at the cynical remark, but once again he knew Dan was right. "And even more important", Dan added, "Your man, Sonny invited us back for all the action we can handle". "He invited you back", Ted quipped. "You know I'm gonna bring you back Ted, we're partners", Dan said with a laugh. When this trip began it was the older and wiser, Ted Lattimore who had all the connections and answers, however, when it ended, it was English Dan, the young dapper twenty-two-year-old, making the decisions and calling the shots.

Ted Lattimore was still steaming, but Dan was too busy counting their earnings. So far the trip had been quite successful. They won twelve hundred in Boston and another fourteen hundred in Harlem. There was not much action in Baltimore that Saturday night. There was one bright moment. It came when Dan ran into one of his old pool shooting buddies, Little Jake. They shot the breeze about North Philly for a few, and the trip came to a quiet end. The Lattimore Oldsmobile sign was a welcoming sight as Dan woke from his slumber. Ted was in a slightly better mood by that time as the road weary duo climbed out of the car. Dan asked to use the bathroom, and as he walked pass the showroom office. He couldn't help but notice an enlarged framed photograph of a young Ted Lattimore and a young Chick Davis. Dan blurted out a laugh having finally unveiled the *mysterious* North Philly and South Philly information channel.

CHAPTER 14

The Cruelty of Time

IT'S BEEN FIVE LONG YEARS since that memorable road trip, as Dan watched everything change right in front of his eyes. He tried desperately to hold on to some of the lifestyle he was accustomed to, and the game he so truly loved. He saw less and less of Ted Lattimore, partially because of the disappearance of pool halls, but mostly because Ted decided to remarry. Dan stopped in to see Chick Davis from time to time, and even his crowd wasn't the same. He pulled up to the curb and parked. The Oldsmobile wasn't new anymore, but Dan kept it clean, besides he would only be a minute.

As the old pool hustlers disappeared, they were replaced with young cats that neither had the skills, nor the heart to be real pool shooters. In fact, one of Dan's older pool buddies was slashed in the face by a young fool, over a lousy ten-dollar bet. Yes, things were definitely changing. However, one thing did not change. Dan still loved to get an early start and this Saturday morning was no different. After his cup of coffee and light breakfast, Dan decided to pay his old friend Sugarfoot a visit. Sugarfoot's Pool Hall was one of the last in North Philly, and there was not much action there anymore, but English Dan wasn't concerned about action, he was just homesick. As he strolled through the door with his cue stick case in hand, he noticed a young slender teenager shooting alone, in the rear of the hall. That sight brought a smile to Dan's faced not only because the young man resembled him as a teen, but he also realized after quick observation, that the young lad could shoot.

"Dan it's been a long time", Sugarfoot greeted him with a hug. The name Dan caught the attention of the young man. "Your name is Dan, are you English Dan?" He asked with excitement. Before Dan could respond, he walked over and shook his hand. "Is it true that you won a brand new car?" Dan just smiled. "They say you bet $25,000 on one game of straight pool, is that true?" Sugarfoot had to come to his rescue. "Settle down son, let the man breathe." Pool hall tales are just like fish tales; they tend to grow bigger with time. The thought of those games made Dan miss those moments even more. He had not seen P.J. Anderson since that night in South Philly. The word on the street is that he went against his father's wishes as predicted, and joined up with Luigi Appellini. When the federal drug agents lowered the boom on their organization, P.J. and Joe-Joe, Louie's lieutenant went to jail. Dan also heard that Willie, P.J's slimy associate was killed in a drug deal gone wrong.

The youngster continued to rattle off questions, but Dan was deep in thought. He wondered as he looked at the teenager, where did all those years go. It was just a minute ago that the young teenager was him, playing hooky from school, learning how to shoot pool, dodging the truant officers and eventually falling in love with the game. Dan's passion and skills would eventually persuade everyone in the game, to fall in love with him. It was around that time someone gave him the moniker *English Dan* and the pool hustlers came calling with bulging pockets. Soon after that, something cruel happened and that cruelty began to twist, distort and reshape his world. A world that for a moment was untouched and un-tampered with. That cruelty has a personal and proper name, and his name is time.

Dan quickly learned that he was no match for that albatross called *time*, so he began to change and make the necessary adjustments that his life demanded at this stage. His deep thoughts were suddenly interrupted by Sugarfoot's bellowing voice. "Hey Dan, there's two cats at the door asking for you." Dan did not turn around immediately because he knew who they were. Instead he reached out and shook the young pool shooters hand and then handed the cue case to him. "A very good man gave this cue to me some time ago. I am now passing it on to you because I no longer have any need for it." Dan's needs had changed and the two gentlemen at the door were the reasons why.

Shortly after his road trip with Ted Lattimore in 1952, Dan made one of the best decisions in his young life. He married Amy, the quiet Burnett sister and the two gentlemen at the door were their two sons. Vincent the older one, smiled as Dan began to walk towards them. There was a twinkle in his eyes that gave Dan a warm comforting feeling inside. The young son, Kevin held tight to his big brother's hand. He wore a curious look on his face as his eyes gazed around the room filled with large very strange looking tables. They were fashionably dressed in warm parkas and buttoned caps to stave off the late autumn air. Amy had grown a little impatient waiting for Dan in the car and sent her two sons to fetch him. That statement is filled with irony, because it was Amy's grace and patience that attracted the young high stakes pool hustler. It was her vision and perception that enabled Dan, to see beyond those long late nights in those smoked-filled pool halls. It was also her brother-in-law who pulled some strings at the Allanwood Steel Mill that allowed Dan, to settle down and properly provide for his family. The transition was not easy for English Dan and he would be the first to admit there was something quite fascinating about his life as a pool hustler, but that was behind him now. As he embraced his two sons at the door, it was time for him to embrace the challenge of raising a family whom he truly loved and a family that was ever expanding. Amy was expecting their third child. It was time to bid farewell to the game he loved as well. High stakes pool hustling in the inner cities has a very special place in the hearts and minds of many. That cruel cat named *time* may have taken away the game, but the memories will live forever. Dan turned slightly, and took one more look at the sign, "Sugarfoot's Pool Room", as Amy quietly said, "Eddie, it's time to go."

AFTERWORD BY ENGLISH DAN

I WAS TAKEN ABACK WHEN Mr. Self first approached me with the idea of writing a book about pool hustlers. As he continued to press me with questions about that era, the excitement returned as if it were yesterday. The more information he demanded, the more I had to revisit those nights, and a tiny spark rekindled that flame in my heart, for a game I once truly loved.

As the halls closed, and the game faded, I think it left many of us broken hearted, so much that I never played the game much after that. Some cats played for *fun*, however for me, the high stakes (cash) and the game are inseparable. The two were interwoven together, and that's what made the game so popular. Ironically speaking, today's players very skillful, but as soon as you mention money, all those skills tend to disappear into thin air.

I do appreciate the current 9-ball tournaments televised on various cable networks. The venues are well orchestrated, and the players, both male and female, put on a dazzling show in front of a very appreciative audience. The prize money makes any of the stakes I pulled down, look like small change. However, when I think of some of the games I played, and the great players I was privileged to see, it still makes me smile.

I'll probably have to work on my game, because as soon as some of these cats read this wonderful story, they're gonna come looking for me again, just like they did over 60 years ago. Some things never change.

English Dan

63 years later, English Dan is still as sharp as ever. He recalls some of the pool halls in the city (Philadelphia) and the surrounding area, and the skillful pool hustlers that crossed their thresholds.

Pool Halls

Chick Davis' Pool Hall, Broad and Rodman Street
Miss Bee's, 19th and Susquehanna Avenue
Black Tom's, 15th and Dauphin Street
Sugarfoot's, Broad and Susquehanna Avenue
18th and Susquehanna Avenue
18th and Norris Street
Woodstock and Norris Street
23rd and Ridge Avenue
61st and Passyunk Avenue
9th and Holland Street
19th and Cheltenham Avenue (**This pool hall has stood the test of time and is still in business today**)

You may wish to visit our website and tell your story or the story of someone you know about and the magical era of high stakes pool hustling in the 1950's.

POOL HUSTLERS

Arthur (Little Augie) Snell
Earl Bantom
"Nine Ball" Jerry
Black Tom
Leonard "Action" Johnson
Steve "Pockets" Larchwood
"Pic Man"
"Can't Miss" Willie
Billy West
"Cue Ball" Charlie
"Little Jake"
Eddie "English Dan" Gordon

P.I.
Charlie McFeel
Daddy Woods
Kacky Joe
"Midnight Blue"
"Young Boy" Larry
"Home Boy"
"Cigar Slim"
"Little Frankie"
LeRoy
Ted Lattimore

Rules of the Game

With the assistance of Eddie "English Dan" Gordon, a few other pool shooters, and "Generation Pool", an online website, we have assembled as list of the many different pool games, and their rules of play. Some of these rules will vary from one hall to the next. We hope this will regenerate interest in the game, for those who no longer play, and introduce this fascinating game to any newcomers.

14.1 – or Continuous Pool – also known as *"Straight Pool"*. This game is not played much anymore. It was very popular in the 1940's and 50's.

Straight pool is played with 15 balls, and each ball, when pocketed counts as one point. The first player to reach the required score, wins. Usually the winning score is 50 points, but sometimes players agree to 100 points. It's called 14.1 because after the first 14 balls are pocketed, those 14 balls are racked, leaving one on the table. When the 15th ball interferes with a new rack, it's placed with the other 14. When the cue ball interferes with the rack, it's placed "in hand" anywhere behind the "string". (You place the cue ball anywhere you wish as long as it is behind the designated marker).

Eight Ball, is still one of your more popular games today. It is also played with 15 balls. The number 8-ball, when racked, is placed in the center.

A striped ball and solid colored ball is placed at each corner. When the designated player breaks the rack, if a solid ball is pocketed (low numbered), those are the balls that the player must pocket. If a striped ball is pocketed (high numbered), that player must pocket the remaining striped balls. When both (high and low) are pocketed on the break, the player has a choice. When no ball is pocketed on the break, the opponent has a choice (open table). If the eight ball is pocketed on the initial break, and no foul occurred (cue ball pocketed at the same time), then that player wins that game.

Now some of your more savvy pool shooters have played many different versions of "8-ball" such as:

Last Pocket – The last pocket the player uses becomes the only pocket that player can pocket the 8-ball.

One Pocket – The two players choose a pocket. The object is to score 8 (any eight) of the 15 balls in the player's target pocket.

Cut-Throat – This game is great to play in social situations. It's usually played with 3 people. Each player chooses 5 balls. The object is to pocket your opponent's balls before the opponent pockets yours.

Nine Ball – We saved "9-ball" of last. In the 1950's, after straight pool and 8-ball faded, this game emerged as the game of choice for the high stakes pool hustlers. When the national and international pool tournaments were created in the 1970's, 9-ball became the only game in town. It's a much faster game, because you are only playing with 9-balls, numbered one through nine.

The object of "9-ball" is to pocket the balls in numerical order, beginning with the one. The player that pockets the ninth and final ball, wins the game. Just like in 8-ball, if the nine ball is pocketed on the break, that player wins the game.

English Dan was proficient in all 3 games, but when asked about his preference, he chose "straight pool". He stated, "In order to be successful at straight pool, you had to have endurance. A lot of cats would tire after a few games." 9-ball was quick and fast, but English Dan always thought that luck interfered with the end result too frequently.

In the Hollywood sequel to the 1961 classic "The Hustler", Eddie Felson played by Paul Newman, "The Color of Money" portrayed an aging Fast Eddie stake horsing a hot shot protégé played by Tom Cruise. He too (Felson) preferred straight pool over 9-ball. Paul Newman would receive an Oscar for that role. Maybe it's time for Hollywood to do yet another classic movie about the fascinating world of high stakes pool hustlers.

Chick Davis, pool hall owner (right side) and
Willie Mosconi, pool great (left side)

ABOUT THE AUTHOR

RAMEL SELF IS THE AUTHOR of Pool Hustlers: The Legend of English Dan. His debut novel based on a true story has the readers salivating for more. There is already some movie chatter about this fascinating story.

Keep an eye out for the sequel and many other projects with his signature on them. Ramel Self was born and raised in South Philadelphia, not too far from Chick's Pool Hall. It was one of many pool halls mentioned in the book.

Ramel Self is available for readings and book signings, contact mekkasiapublishing@comcast.net

Made in the USA
Las Vegas, NV
17 February 2021